MW00561644

DISABILITY AND TEACHING

Disability and Teaching highlights issues of disability in K-12 schooling faced by teachers, who are increasingly accountable for the achievement of all students regardless of the labels assigned to them. It is designed to engage prospective and practicing teachers in examining their personal theories and beliefs about disability and education.

Part I offers four case studies dealing with issues such as inclusion, over-representation in special education, teacher assumptions and biases, and the struggles of novice teachers. These cases illustrate the need to understand disability and teaching within the contexts of school, community, and the broader society and in relation to other contemporary issues facing teachers. Each is followed by space for readers to write their own reactions and reflections, educators' dialogue about the case, space for readers' reactions to the educators' dialogue, a summary, and additional questions. Part II presents public arguments representing different views about the topic: conservative, liberal-progressive, and disability centered. Part III situates the authors' personal views within the growing field of Disability Studies in Education and provides exercises for further reflection and a list of resources.

Disability and Teaching is the 8th volume in the Reflective Teaching and the Social Conditions of Schooling Series, edited by Daniel P. Liston and Kenneth M. Zeichner. This series of small, accessible, interactive texts introduces the notion of teacher reflection and develops it in relation to the social conditions of schooling. Each text focuses on a specific issue or content area in relation to teaching and follows the same format. Books in this series are appropriate for teacher education courses across the curriculum.

Susan L. Gabel is Professor and Director, Doctoral Program in Education, Chapman University, USA.

David J. Connor is Associate Professor of Special Education/Learning Disabilities, Hunter College/City University of New York, USA.

**REFLECTIVE TEACHING AND THE
SOCIAL CONDITIONS OF SCHOOLING**
A Series for Prospective and Practicing Teachers
Daniel P. Liston and Kenneth M. Zeichner, Series Editors

DISABILITY AND TEACHING

Susan L. Gabel and David J. Connor

Routledge
Taylor & Francis Group

NEW YORK AND LONDON

First published 2014
by Routledge
711 Third Avenue, New York, NY 10017

Simultaneously published in the UK
by Routledge
2 Park Square, Milton Park, Abingdon, Oxon OX14 4RN

Routledge is an imprint of the Taylor & Francis Group, an informa business

© 2014 Taylor & Francis

The right of the editor to be identified as the author of the editorial material, and of the authors for their individual chapters, has been asserted in accordance with sections 77 and 78 of the Copyright, Designs and Patents Act 1988.

All rights reserved. No part of this book may be reprinted or reproduced or utilized in any form or by any electronic, mechanical, or other means, now known or hereafter invented, including photocopying and recording, or in any information storage or retrieval system, without permission in writing from the publishers.

Trademark notice: Product or corporate names may be trademarks or registered trademarks, and are used only for identification and explanation without intent to infringe.

Library of Congress Cataloging in Publication Data
Gabel, Susan L. (Susan Lynn), 1956-
Disability and teaching / by Susan l. Gabel and David J. Connor.
    pages cm. — (Reflective teaching and the social conditions of schooling)
    Includes bibliographical references and index.
    1. People with disabilities—Education—Case studies.   I. Connor, D. J.   II. Title.
    LC4019.G33 2014
    371.9—dc23

                                                        2013005509

ISBN: 978–0–415–81398–3 (hbk)
ISBN: 978–0–8058–4914–1 (pbk)
ISBN: 978–0–203–79683–2 (ebk)

Typeset in Times New Roman
by RefineCatch Limited, Bungay, Suffolk, UK

SUSTAINABLE
FORESTRY
INITIATIVE

Certified Sourcing
www.sfiprogram.org
SFI-00555
The SFI label applies to the text stock.

Printed and bound in the United States of America by
Walsworth Publishing Company, Marceline, MO.

To David:
Teacher, scholar, colleague, friend, passionate activist and co-conspirator.
Without you, this book would not have been completed.
– SG

To Gary, Robert, Lisa, and Kim:
with love from Big Bruv.
– DC

CONTENTS

II.   PUBLIC ARGUMENTS   *79*

III.   A FINAL ARGUMENT, AND SOME SUGGESTIONS AND RESOURCES FOR FURTHER REFLECTION   *111*

SERIES PREFACE

INTRODUCTION

We know that some readers tend to skip introductory material, but we hope you will continue. The success of this book depends, in large part, on how you use it. Here we outline some of our key assumptions and suggest ways to approach the material in each book of our series, "Reflective Teaching and the Social Conditions of Schooling." First we identify some of the reasons for creating this series. We then relate a bit about our dissatisfaction with how teacher education has been conducted and how it could be changed. Finally we suggest ways to utilize best the material in this and subsequent texts.

Two decades ago we were asked to develop further the ideas outlined in our book *Teacher Education and the Social Conditions of Schooling* (Liston & Zeichner, 1991). It was suggested that we take our basic approach to teacher reflection and our ideas about teacher education curricula and put them into practice. The proposal was attractive and the subsequent endeavor proved to be very challenging. It never seems easy to translate educational "shoulds" and possibilities into schooling "cans" and realities. But over the last fifteen years we have made progress in that effort by designing a book series intended to help prospective, beginning, and experienced teachers reflect on their profession, their teaching, and their experiences. We are pleased and delighted to have the opportunity to share this work with you. We hope you will find these texts engaging and useful.

We are two university teacher educators, both former elementary teachers, who have worked in inner-city, small town, and suburban elementary and middle schools. For the last twenty years we have worked with prospective and practicing teachers, examined the changing terrain of teacher education, and suggested and argued for ways to better prepare teachers for our public schools. We are committed to public schools as democratic institutions, as places of learning in which people of all walks of life come to learn how to live together in a democratic society. Although we are personally committed to ways of working and living together that are much more collaborative than exist today—we are educators first, realists second, and dreamers third. It is our firm belief that an education that engages prospective and practicing teachers' heads and hearts, their beliefs and passions, their hopes and instructional practices needs to be fair and honest. We have not written or sponsored these texts to convince you to see schools and society as we do but rather to engage you in a consideration of crucial issues that all teachers need to address. Once engaged we hope that you will be better able to articulate your views, responses, and responsibilities to students and parents, and come to better understand aspects of your role as a teacher in a democratic society.

IMPACTS OF THE SOCIAL CONDITIONS OF SCHOOLING

Prospective teachers need to be prepared for the problems and challenges of public schooling. When we initiated this series we observed that all too often the focus in schools (departments and colleges) of education remained strictly on the processes that occur within the K-12 classroom and inside the school walls. At that time many teacher education programs emphasized instructional methodology and the psychology of the learner in university course work and underscored survival strategies during student teaching. These were and are certainly important elements in any teacher's preparation and ones that cannot be ignored. But classrooms and schools are not insulated environments. What goes on inside schools is greatly influenced by what occurs outside of schools. These teacher preparation programs gave scant attention to the social, political, and cultural contexts of schooling. Today's professional preparation has changed in some significant ways, however much has stayed the same.

Many teacher educators now recognize that the students who attend and the teachers and administrators who work within our public schools bring into the school building all sorts of cultural assumptions, social influences, and contextual dynamics. Many teacher educators understand that unless dilemmas of schooling. In schools of education we have tended to teach what sociologists or philosophers of education have to say about schools, without adequately connecting these observations and findings to teachers' struggles and everyday dilemmas. This more academic framing limits prospective teachers' acquaintance and engagement with the social conditions of schooling. Recently even these academically inclined social foundations courses have been eliminated from or drastically curtailed within university-based and alternative teacher education programs. We want to reassert the importance of these contextual and value-laden issues within teacher preparation. In our work with prospective and practicing teachers we have developed ways to examine contextual issues of schooling and to enable them to articulate their ideas, beliefs, theories, and feelings about those issues. The books in this series utilize some of these insights and pass along to others the content and the processes we have found useful.

When students and faculty engage in discussions of the social and political conditions of schooling and the effects of these conditions on students and schools, it is likely that the talk will be lively and controversies will emerge. In this arena there are no absolutely "right" or "wrong" answers. There are choices, frequently difficult ones, choices that require considerable discussion, deliberation, and justification. In order for these discussions to occur we need to create classroom settings that are conducive to conversations about difficult and controversial issues. We have found that the best format for such discussion is not the debate, the (in)formal argument, or dispassionate and aloof analysis. Instead the most conducive environment is a classroom designed to create dialogue and conversation among participants with differing points of view. There isn't a recipe or formula that will ensure this type of environment but we think the following suggestions are worth considering.

It is important for individuals using these texts to engage in discussions that are sensitive and respectful toward others, and at the same time challenge each other's views. This is not an easy task. It requires each participant to come to the class sessions prepared, to listen attentively to other people's views, and to address one another with a tone and attitude of respect. This means that when disagreements among individuals occur, and they inevitably will occur, each participant should find ways to express that disagreement without diminishing or attacking other individuals. Participants in these professional discussions need to be able to voice their views freely and to be sensitive toward others. Frequently, this is difficult to do. In discussions of controversial issues, ones that strike emotional chords, we are prone to argue in a way that belittles or disregards another person and their point of view. At times, we try to dismiss both the claim and the person. But if the discussions that these books help to initiate are carried on in that demeaning fashion, the potential power of these works will not be realized. A discussion of this paragraph should occur before discussion of the substance raised by this particular text. It is our conviction that when a class keeps both substance and pedagogy in the forefront it has a way of engaging individuals in a much more positive manner. From our own past experiences we have found that during the course of a class's use of this material it may be quite helpful to pause and focus on substantive and pedagogical issues in a conscious and forthright manner. Such time is generally well spent.

UNDERSTANDING AND EXAMINING PERSONAL BELIEFS ABOUT TEACHING AND SCHOOLING

It is also our belief that many educational issues engage and affect our heads and our hearts. Teaching is work that entails both thinking and feeling and those who can reflectively think and feel will find their work more rewarding and their efforts more successful. Good teachers find ways to listen and to integrate their passions, beliefs, and judgments. And so we encourage not only the type of group deliberation just outlined, but also an approach to reading that is attentive to an individual's felt sense or what some might call "gut" level reactions. In the books in this series that contain case material and written reactions to that material, along with the public arguments that pertain to the issues raised, we believe it is essential that you attend to your felt reactions and attempt to sort out what those reactions tell you. At times it seems we can predict our reactions to the readings and discussions of this material while at other times it can invoke responses and feelings that surprise us. Attending to those issues in a heartfelt manner, one that is honest and forthright, gives us a better sense of ourselves as teachers and our understandings of the world. Not only do students walk into schools with expectations and assumptions formed as a result of life experiences but so do their teachers. Practicing and prospective teachers can benefit from thinking about their expectations and assumptions. Hopefully, our work in this book series will facilitate this sort of reflection.

ABOUT THE BOOKS IN THIS SERIES

In the first work in this series, *Reflective Teaching: An Introduction—2nd Edition*, we discuss and amplify the notion of teacher reflection and connect it to the social conditions of schooling. Reflection is an often used and frequently abused idea and we hope this text capably grounds teachers' and teacher educators' understanding of this professional practice. Building on this concept in the second work of the series, *Culture and Teaching* (Liston and Zeichner), we encourage reflection on and examination of issues connected to teaching in a culturally diverse society. In *Gender and Teaching* Frances (Frinde) Mayer and Janie Ward invite readers to examine the ways in which gender is a difference that makes a difference in our schools and classrooms. In *Linguistic Diversity and Teaching* Nancy Commins and Ofelia Miramontes explore the linguistic, cultural, class, and ethnic aspects of language use in our schools. In *Reading and Teaching* Richard Meyer and Maryann Manning delve into the nuances of literacy instruction. In *Religion and Teaching* Ronald Anderson uncovers and illustrates the various places religion appears in U.S. schools. In *Mathematics and Teaching* Michele Crockett explores the intersection of culture and mathematics instruction. And in *Disability and Teaching* Susan Gabel and David Connor highlight issues of disability in K-12 schooling.

What makes this series and these works unique is that each one takes as its central concern the reflective examination of our educational practices—set within the social, political, cultural, and structural aspects of teaching and schooling. All of the texts (except for *Reflective Teaching* and *Reading and Teaching*) employ constructed case studies, and actual reader responses and reactions so as to portray, tease out, and illuminate the variety of issues and interpretations that teachers, parents, and administrators see in and bring to this material. In addition to the case studies these texts elaborate the various "public arguments" employed (by editorialists, scholars, and community members) to support very different educational paths, values, and directions. Readers will find themselves agreeing more with one public argument than another. We hope you seriously consider the other viewpoints and differing case responses. It is crucial that the reader understands each of these viewpoints and begins to articulate his or her own response. As we noted at the beginning of this preface we have not written these texts to convince you to see schools and society as we do but rather to engage you in a consideration of some of the critical issues that all teachers should address.

SERIES ACKNOWLEDGMENTS

Two individuals have been essential to the conception and execution of this series. Kathleen Keller, our first editor at St. Martin's Press (where the series originated), initially suggested that we further develop the ideas outlined in *Teacher Education and the Social Conditions of Schooling* (Liston & Zeichner, 1991). Kathleen was very helpful in the initial stages of this effort. Naomi Silverman, our current and beloved editor—first at Lawrence Erlbaum Associates and now at Routledge, has patiently and skillfully prodded us along attending to both the "big picture" and the small details. We are thankful and indebted to Naomi for her yearly AERA brunches/lunches, and the opportunity to pursue both the thoughtful and practical in teaching and schooling. We are quite fortunate to have developed this working relationship and friendship with Naomi.

Daniel P. Liston and Kenneth M. Zeichner

PREFACE

At first glance, the title of this book might suggest that it is about special education for special education teachers. On one level this is true, since the book does, indeed, address some of the most basic issues and problems facing special education today. Yet, general educators find disabled students[1] in their classrooms every year and they increasingly are accountable for the achievement of *all* students, regardless of disability labels assigned to them. So this book is also about general education for general education teachers. We hope that it demonstrates that the most basic issues and problems facing special education are the same as those facing general education. In other words, this book has been conceived and written as a book about teaching for people who are or who want to be teachers.

The words "disability" and "teaching" sometimes conjure up images of instruction by specialists in individualization, collaboration between teachers with differing expertise, and support systems for teachers and their students

---

1 We have deliberately used the phrase "disabled students," as opposed to wording "students with disabilities." In disability rights history, it is important to note that the latter phrase was seen as a major breakthrough in emphasizing "people first" language that deemphasized disability and emphasized personhood. On the other hand, our choice of phrase is purposefully political as it emphasizes power relations among groups in society, and stresses how physical barriers, institutional structures, and pervasive beliefs literally cause the disabling of people with physical, cognitive, emotional, or sensory impairments. In this sense, disability is something that happens to people, it is a social wrong. It is not something inherently wrong with an individual.

who struggle to achieve. On the other hand, for many people, the words bring to mind segregated classrooms, Individual Educational Plans and bureaucratic paperwork, and infeasible accountability for students who "can't learn," "drain the system," "water down the curriculum," and "shouldn't be there." Regardless of the associations one brings to the terms, differing ideas about the relationship between disability and teaching have always produced ongoing debates. The debates speak to the most basic set of beliefs about K-12 education—the purposes and conditions of schooling in a democratic society. Some of these debates are the focus of this book. For example, in what ways are disability, race, class, and gender related? In what ways does widespread bias influence beliefs about students, and who is disabled as a result of policy or practice resulting from bias? The first two cases explore these questions. In addition, all four cases struggle with the following questions: How can teaching *disable* students and, likewise, how can it *enable* students? How do teachers' responses to policy shape the experiences of disabled students? What kind of schools and classroom communities are in the best interest of individual students or society-at-large? Who benefits when disabled students are in general education classrooms and who benefits when they are in segregated classrooms? Finally, who gets to make the decisions about how laws and policies are interpreted, whose "best interests" are served, and who is left out of the decision-making process? These are just some of the questions that are raised and explored by the cases in this book.

The Reflective Teaching book series encourages teachers to examine their personal theories and beliefs. In the second book in the series, *Culture and Teaching*, Daniel Liston and Kenneth Zeichner (1996) write that theories and beliefs "are formed and arise from our past experiences, our received knowledge, and our basic values. Part of reflective teaching entails an introspective and critical analysis of those experiences, understandings, and values" (p. xviii). Introspection sometimes reveals attitudes or values that one does not know exist but that have been firmly instantiated by personal experience and countless interactions with popular culture. These tacit beliefs serve as guides for behavior even though there is no conscious recognition of them. The case studies in this book are designed to help the reader uncover and question the attitudes, values, or beliefs that s/he holds about disability, to explore alternatives, and consider the consequences of each perspective.

Understanding oneself and one's beliefs as well as the beliefs of others is only the first step. This book also hopes to encourage the reader to contemplate the actions that such understanding requires. If you are a practicing teacher, how do your understandings inform your teaching? Likewise, how do new understandings serve to potentially transform your teaching? If you are a new or prospective teacher, how does changing your ideas about teaching impact your view of a teacher's roles and responsibilities? In turn, what commitments can you make as a result of changing perspectives? Hopefully, you are reading this book with colleagues or in a university classroom with other students. What are your peers' views and how do they affect your ideas? In what ways might you contribute to learning of your peers? In sum, to what degree are you going to change as a result of reading and responding to this book

In the third book in this series, *Gender and Teaching*, Frances Maher and Janie Ward (2002) ask whether gender is "a difference that makes a difference" (p. xv). We are not sure whether it is useful to pose the same question about disability: Is disability a difference that makes a difference? We suspect that most educators would agree that it does, but we hope you will still pose the question to your fellow students, colleagues, and mentors to learn what they have to say. Better yet, pose the question to the disabled people you know. We know that many disabled people would also say that disability is a difference that makes a difference, if only because of the importance of viewing and valuing diversity in our society. There are also those who argue that disability makes a difference because it reveals otherwise hidden assumptions about the purposes of schooling, such as who "fits" into our society. Of course, disability makes a difference when environments or programs create barriers that prevent people from full participation in school. In such cases, we find some students entering and exiting schools through separate doorways, sitting in isolated classrooms, or even attending segregated schools where they are sent because they "don't belong," "can't handle," or "won't learn" in integrated settings. We certainly could draw historical and sociological analogies between gender, class, sexual orientation, or race discrimination and disability discrimination. Each of these social groups has experienced barriers that prevent or have prevented them from equal access to a quality education. Historically, disabled people have been hidden at home, sent to asylums or other institutions, segregated from the mainstream of society, separated from family, neighborhood, and community. In the recent past in the US—pre-1975—disabled children were not even guaranteed a free public education. In the late twentieth and early twenty-first century, disabled children still do not have the unmitigated freedom to attend their neighborhood school or general education classrooms. They can be sent to a school an hour or more away and they can be segregated in separate classrooms away from nondisabled students. This does not always happen, but it is still commonplace for many children. Even today, most students with significant cognitive impairment, or what was once called mental retardation, continue to experience discrimination and segregation to a startling degree (Smith, 2010).

We are very mindful of the word "different," as it begs the unasked question of "different from *what*?" In this case, it would mean "normal children." Herein lies an important premise of this book: we hope you will think deeply about who is considered "normal," and conversely, who is viewed as "abnormal," along with the many implications for all teachers and children. In brief, a better question for this book to ask might be: *What kind of difference does disability make?*

This question immediately gives rise to a host of others. For example: How does disability alter social contexts? How do disabled students influence school communities? In what ways do schools or communities disable or enable students? How does their presence reflect or change the purposes of schooling? In what ways are teaching practices "normed" because of disability? In what ways is disability what it is because of particular, arguably limited, approaches to teaching? These are perhaps more difficult questions to answer because they are questions that get at the heart of the social construction of disability, revealing uncomfortable realities about the social conditions of schooling.

In Part III, when we share our own views, you will find that our perspective is that disability is, indeed, socially constructed. If this is a new idea to you, allow us to explain briefly what we mean by this. When we say that disability is socially constructed, we mean that society is organized in ways that create barriers to full participation by some of its citizens. Barriers *disable* some people by excluding them. For disabled people, obstacles to participation in society can include lack of: equal access to general education classes and curriculum; competitive employment opportunities; options of where and with whom to live; choice to express one's sexuality; access to opportunities for marriage and family building. Generally speaking, those disabled by exclusionary practices are people who have impairments or functional limitations of some kind, but later we will see that things are not as simple as that. One of the things we hope to make you more aware of is ways in which "disability" is socially constructed through cultural discourses. In other words, how does what we know as disability come to be? What are the forces at play in society that shape our beliefs and understanding about signifying certain types of differences among humans as disabilities? You will see examples of cultural discourses in each of the case studies in this book.

CONTENT AND STRUCTURE

Consistent with previous books in this series, this text is organized into three parts. In Part I, the four cases are presented with reactions from prospective and practicing teachers, administrators, parents, teacher educators, and community members. In Part II these four cases are examined in light of three public arguments: conservative, progressive, and disability-centered. Finally, in Part III, we give our own interpretation of the cases and leave the reader with some concluding thoughts.

PART I: THE CASE STUDIES

All of the cases in Part I are derived from our years of experience as special education teachers. We have constructed each one from a collection of experiences and while each case is a compilation, everything actually happened to us or around us when we were practicing special education teachers. On television they say, "The names are changed but the story is true." Likewise, the cases in this book—the names, locations, and minor details are changed or reconfigured, but the fundamental reality and lessons of each case are essentially the same.

Part I focuses on what is happening in schools and what educators (including you) have to say about it. You could think of Part I as using a camera with a zoom lens that zeros in on a particular aspect of the land-scape of schooling. As previously mentioned, the case studies are designed to tackle what we consider to be some of the most basic issues and problems related to disability and teaching today. Case 1, "Inclusion Tension," we find teachers and parents reacting to the district-wide policy about inclusion of disabled students in general education classrooms. The policy is the result of district concerns that special education students need access to the general education curriculum in order to do well on standardized tests that determine whether or not the school is making progress and remains eligible for continued federal funding. The teachers, in particular, worry about how the policy impacts their work and question the value of inclusion. The case explores the meaning of inclusive education, what it takes to succeed or fail at inclusion, the relationship between general and special educators, and the relationship of school to community. Case 2, "Ableism at Forest Run Elementary," explores the ways in which teacher beliefs influence the way teachers make decisions about students and uncovers the ways in which teacher notions of what counts as evidence can lead to discriminatory teacher behavior. This case starts with an actual conversation Susan had with a colleague when she was a public school teacher and includes other examples from her experiences as a teacher educator. We ask you to explore the ways in which students can be stig-matized by the way teachers think and talk about them. In Case 3, "Race,

Place, and the Search for Solutions," we find a school and its community engaged in the debates about the intersections of race, class, and disability. At the center of the case, is a school principal trying to bring the community together to find solutions to problems of resources and low achievement. The challenges facing this school are similar to those facing many under-resourced, urban centers in the US. Observing and contemplating the situation is a new teacher who wonders about the options and whether any solutions are forthcoming. In Case 4, "*Special* Educator?", we find Martin struggling with his new identity as a teacher when he realizes that even though he teaches middle school social studies, he has special education students in his classes. Feeling unprepared and somewhat resentful, Martin works with his mentor and a special education colleague to come to terms with his role as a teacher of *all* students and the strategies needed to support students with diverse abilities.

At the end of each case study, there is space for you to write your reactions. After that, you will find reactions we have gathered from practicing teachers, prospective teachers, administrators, parents, teacher educators, and community members, along with the opportunity to compare your own reactions to theirs. While the reactions represent a wide range of perspectives, please remember that there are many other possibilities—too many to include—and you might have some ideas that are not represented in this book. Following these reactions, there is space for you to write again and after that, we wrap up with a summary and leave you with some questions to ponder. The purpose of this structure is to encourage you to take more than one opportunity to reflect upon and respond to the case studies, to compare your responses to those of others, and to contemplate the ways in which your ideas have evolved over time and after input from others. You could think of this as a series of conversations where each new voice adds layers of complexity and subtlety to the issues raised within the case study. When it comes to your responses to these cases, remember that there are multiple possibilities inherent in each situation. We are interested in having you determine what is *your* position on each case? And, to what degree can you open yourself to other possibilities?

PART II: THE PUBLIC ARGUMENTS

To use the photography metaphor again, Part II takes the zoom off the "camera" that allows a close up of a specific aspect of schooling and replaces it with a view of the entire panorama of education, a "wide shot," so to speak. Think of this section as taking a snapshot of the landscape of schooling using three different panoramas—traditional (or conservative), liberal-progressive (or moderate), and disability-centered (or radical)— each of which filters the view in significantly different ways. Every snapshot offers a distinct way of understanding and explaining the issues represented in the cases. In their book, *Gender and Teaching*, Maher and Ward (2002) write that the "public arguments or 'public voices' represent clusters of orientations organized around general values rather than sets of hard-and-fast principles to which all who speak in that 'voice' must adhere" (p. xviii). The same authors caution us to read the public arguments while understanding it is difficult for a snapshot to reveal the nuance and complexity of a set of values or assumptions from which experiences are interpreted and decisions are generated. The intention of Part II is to introduce you to the variety of approaches to thinking about and acting upon the issues in the case studies. It must be understood that these approaches are much more complex than they can be described here in a single case study book.

The terms "conservative" and "liberal" or "progressive" seem to have lost meaning in recent years. Previous books in this series, by Liston and Zeichner (1996) and Maher and Ward (2002), used the terms to refer to political orientations and we also have chosen to do that. In doing so, there is a risk of reducing these orientations to stereotypes, one-dimensional representations that oversimplify complicated issues. For example, there are many instances of conservatives' support of disability rights and liberals' perpetuation of ableism making it impossible to categorize one position as the "right" one. For example, George H. W. Bush, a president many would consider a political conservative, was a major proponent of the Americans with Disabilities Act. In addition, many disability rights advocates are against physician assisted suicide, a position most often associated with political conservatives. It is important to understand that one's orientation in disability issues only generally correlates with one's political orientation.

What, then, differentiates conservative from liberal or progressive views toward disability? We have chosen a simple way of thinking about the terms. We use conservative to mean a traditional or conventional orientation toward disability, disability policy, and institutional practices. In this view, conservatively oriented individuals might prefer to uphold educational structures, policies, and organizations that maintain separate general and special education, as is found in public schools today. In other words, we are using conservative to mean the *conservation* of tradition. Alternately, progressively oriented individuals would seek reform or change that upholds liberal values of equal access, inclusion, and multiculturalism. This orientation would make one more likely to support inclusive education and thinking of disability as socially constructed, for example. Since these terms and the orientations they describe are being generalized, you probably will find that you and those with whom you are reading this book will cross from one orientation to the other, depending on the issue at hand. Personal experience is often what informs one's position in such situations. You may also have noticed that what counts as progressive in one historical period becomes conservative or conventional in a subsequent period. For example, Public Law 94-142, the Education of the Handicapped Act (EHA) of 1975, was progressive for its time but in our discussion of the disability-centered public argument, the EHA and its more recent reauthorizations (Individuals with Disabilities Education Improvement Act of 2004) will be viewed as conservative.

The complexities of categorizing positions as conservative or progressive will be evident in our discussion of disability policies in Part II, in the third public argument—the radical disability-centered position. This public argument emerges from the disability rights movement of the last fifty years and maintains that disability must be understood within its social, historical, and political contexts and that in our attempts to understand, we must privilege what disabled people have to say about disability. Privileging what disabled people have to say means that we allow their voices, their stories, and their perspectives to be foremost in the process of how we make sense of things when it comes to disability and teaching. As the activist Jim Charlton (2000) simply states, there should be "Nothing about us without us" (p. 3). The philosopher Bat Ami Bar On (1993) says that understanding things from the perspective of those who are at the margins of society is more informative about that society than the perspective of the majority groups who benefit most. The disability-centered public argument, then, positions the phenomenon of disability, disabled people, and what they have to say as the focus of the debate.

PART III: FINAL ARGUMENTS, SOME SUGGESTIONS, AND FURTHER READING

In Part III, we offer our own reading of the issues related to disability and teaching and encourage you to continue to explore this topic by sharing some suggestions and some further readings. In this section, it will be emphasized that the issues and problems associated with disability and teaching are larger and more complex than disability alone. They are entangled with race, gender, class, and other identity markers. Other complicating factors enter into the picture as well. For example, schools differ widely in their available resources. Students who attend these schools experience variable opportunities to learn—some have more opportunities than others. Teachers operate in a world where inequality is built into the very structure of society. Bearing these things in mind, we invoke the perennial question: What can a single teacher do to make a difference in the lives of students? As always, the answer depends on many factors, including whether or not the teacher has prior experience in thinking about the social issues facing schools today. This book is not intended to provide answers as much as to invoke questions and reflection on what one might face as a teacher and how one might respond based on values and beliefs. What kind of difference does disability make for you as a teacher? We hope you will find answers to that question as you read this book and respond to the case studies.

ACKNOWLEDGMENTS

We would like to thank the series editors, Dan Liston and Ken Zeichner, for including this book in their series and for their patience in waiting for its completion. Additional thanks to Naomi Silverman for her support and encouragement through the process. We are both grateful to the disabled students we have taught and the pre-service teachers who've been in our classes. From you, we have learned valuable lessons about disability and teaching.

Susan would like to thank her children—Bob, Tiffany, April, Ben—for reminding her on a daily basis the importance of understanding the difference that disability makes and her husband—Peter—for the journey they have shared.

David would like to thank his family in the UK for being inclusive of all our members.

I

CASE STUDIES AND REACTIONS

INTRODUCTION TO CASE 1

When referring to *inclusive education*, people think of many different things. For some, the phrase brings to mind racial desegregation and culturally responsive teaching. For others, it means that classrooms and schools are communities full of students who represent diversity of gender, race, ethnicity, or sexual orientation. Still others consider education inclusive when students who speak languages other than English are in classrooms with their English-speaking peers. Inclusive education also refers to the movement to have disabled students educated in the general education classroom and to have their support services provided without removing them from the classroom. The latter is the concept of inclusion to which this case refers but as you continue to read the cases in this book, you will see that it is quite difficult to separate the various meanings of inclusion because it is difficult to separate out disability, race, gender, class, and other categories with which people are identified.

In this first case, we find a district and one of its schools confronting the benefits and challenges of inclusive education. The assumptions and beliefs of a variety of stakeholders, or people who have a vested interest in the situation, emerge in the ensuing conversations involving administrators and teachers. The case stirs up many questions about inclusive education. If achievement is the goal of inclusion, does inclusion work? What may be other reasons to be inclusive? Who gets to decide whether or

1

not and when a school or district should implement inclusion? Do disabled students have the right to an inclusive education with their non-disabled peers? On the other hand, should some students have to qualify to be in the general education classroom? Do teachers have a right to exclude some students and if so, on what basis? Do parents of non-disabled students have the right to ask for their child to be transferred out of an inclusive classroom? These are just a few of the questions raised by this case.

As you read, consider the question of who gets to decide whether or not, when, and where inclusion takes place. Some of the educators in the case are skeptical and worry that disabled students will take too much of the teacher's time away from non-disabled students. General education teachers often worry about what they consider to be their lack of expertise in teaching disabled students. It is important, however, to consider from where these beliefs originate. Do they originate in lack of experience or lack of confidence in one's skills and fear of failure? Do they come from resistance to change or, perhaps, from unfounded fears of difference? Do teacher education programs reinforce stereotypic views of two types of educator: general and special? How can teachers meet all the demands placed upon them while also accommodating students with significant learning needs? Are these concerns realistic and if so, are there solutions to them?

CASE 1: "INCLUSION TENSION"

Villa Nueva is a large school district in the southwest. For many years, the district maintained a continuum of special education services. This means that when students are found eligible for special education services, several support options have been available, including full or part-time in the general education classroom, full time in a special education classroom in a neighborhood school, or even attendance at a segregated school where all students have disabilities. However, when Dr. Flores, the new Director of Special Education, came to the district five years ago he persuaded the district administration that the best way to improve overall test scores and assure that schools meet the requirements for annual progress would be to have a policy of full inclusion of all students. By this he meant that all students should be in the general education classroom full time and that any support services required would be provided there. Three years ago the policy was changed and since then, almost every student with an Individual Educational Plan (IEP) is in a general education classroom full time. Special education support services are provided in the general education setting, usually by general and special educators co-teaching together.

At a January meeting with elementary principals, Dr. Flores displays a chart showing a comparison of district-wide elementary test results over the last four years (See Table 1.1).

Several of the principals remind Dr. Flores of his claim that inclusion would help the district meet goals for annual progress yet the gains in achievement test results could alternatively be explained by the shifts in curriculum and instruction emphasis in the district. They also point out that although gains were made, they have been insufficient to meet state and national requirements. In sum, the problems caused by inclusion seem to have outweighed these gains.

"Inclusion has created a lot of difficulties for my teachers and it seems to have given us little in return," one principal says. "Think of all the time it takes away from the general education students."

His colleague, Dr. Simmons, Principal of Villa Nueva Elementary School, adds, "I agree that it appears we have too little to show if we're only measuring success by district level test results. I wonder if there's another measure we should be using, as well?"

"I understand that these broad scale data may not be very sensitive to what's happening at the school level, but these are the data that Dr. Flores claimed would be impacted by inclusion," responds the first principal.

Table 1.1 Percentage of Students Meeting or Exceeding Targets in Standardized Testing

%	Year 1	Year 2	Year 3	Year 4
95–100				
90–94				
85–89		X	X	X
80–84	X			
75–79				
70–74				
65–69				
60–64				
55–59				
50–54				

Dr. Flores interjects, "Yes, I did make the case that inclusion would likely boost our overall test scores, and it has. There has been some increase but I also wonder if anyone has observed some benefits that can't be measured by standardized tests?"

"I propose that we all go back to our schools and collect some information that might prove useful in making decisions," Dr. Simmons suggests. "I am willing to poll my teachers and parents and study other kinds of evidence. For example, I'm interested in individual achievement levels of my students with IEPs. I wonder if they have shown individual gains."

Dr. Flores responds, "Yes, that's a good idea. And we might also try to find out if teachers, students, and parents have other things to tell us—such as how has inclusion changed classrooms and the school in general? And what level of commitment has everyone made to inclusion?"

As the principals leave the meeting to return to their buildings, Dr. Simmons ponders the situation at his school. Villa Nueva Elementary is one of five elementary schools in the district. Like many other district schools, 75% of its students are Hispanic and bilingual and a large percentage of them are receiving support from the district English as a Second Language (ESL) office. The rest of the student population is African American (20%) and White (5%). While driving to his building, Dr. Simmons thinks about the students who have IEPs—89% of them are Hispanic and 8% are African American. Most of the Hispanic students with IEPs are still learning English. While he had thought about this before, Dr. Simmons is now feeling a bit incredulous and wondering if his staff is confusing English Language Learners with students who have impairments. He decides to try to find out.

During the following week, Dr. Flores and Jennifer Jones, the special education teacher in his building, examine the files of each student at Villa Nueva who has an IEP. They study grades, achievement test results, report cards, and anecdotal evidence in each student's cumulative file, and compare these data over the course of the last four years. Where there are questions, they talk with individual teachers to learn more.

At the next faculty meeting, Dr. Simmons describes the analysis process in which he and Ms. Jones have been engaged. Teachers are curious about the results. "Before we discuss what we have learned," he notes, "I would like to talk about inclusion as a philosophy. We've been doing inclusion as a means to a particular end—for the purpose of increasing achievement scores. However, I want to know if there are other good reasons to practice inclusion." He then remains quiet and waits for teachers to share their ideas.

"I think inclusion could be understood as a philosophy," Mrs. Rivera tentatively proposes. "As a philosophy it would be something done because we value diversity and want students to grow up knowing how to live peaceably in a diverse society."

Another teacher adds, "I suppose it's true that we should value diversity yet how do we know that the benefits of inclusion outweigh the problems? Inclusion certainly makes our job harder. It's more work. I wasn't trained to teach those kids."

"We could say that about a lot of things," responds Mrs. Sandy Leary. "If we're going to separate some students because they learn differently, then are we going to separate other students because they look different? Since I've been working with Jennifer on inclusion I've noticed a change in my students. They are more accepting of individual differences. I think I am more accepting, too."

Another teacher counters, "Well, accepting individual differences is a good thing, but it doesn't address the pressure for improving achievement scores. What's more important? What keeps the money flowing to our school and all of us gainfully employed—accepting differences or increasing achievement scores?"

Mrs. Rivera adds, "There is the issue of labeling students who should not be labeled. Without inclusion, many of those students would be segregated into special education classrooms. I'm talking about the Spanish speaking students."

"Mrs. Rivera is correct," adds Dr. Simmons. "We do have the problem of over-identifying Spanish speaking children when it comes to special education."

Ms. Jones adds, "So inclusion allows children who are incorrectly identified to remain in the general education classroom. Are there other benefits?"

"We've come up with some interesting claims for and against inclusion as a philosophy," concludes Dr. Simmons. "On the pro side, there is the acceptance of diversity, preparing children for life in a diverse society, and counteracting mistakes in identification. On the con side, there is the basic challenge of doing inclusion and the possibility that it doesn't sufficiently raise district- or school-wide achievement test scores, and may make teachers work harder."

Several teachers at once press Dr. Simmons for the results of his analysis of the progress of students with IEPs. "I'm not ready to share those results yet," he says. "I think I will have the final analysis ready at our next meeting."

Some teachers moan, wishing they had been given answers. "Oh, and one more thing," adds Dr. Simmons. "Until we meet again, I would like you to think about two more questions. Number one, who should get to decide whether or not we practice inclusion? And number two, what are the criteria for deciding?"

As teachers leave the meeting, Ms. Jones overhears Mrs. Rivera talking with two other teachers. They appear to disagree about the answers to Dr. Simmons' questions. Mrs. Rivera says she thinks the Parent Organization should be involved in the decision. Another teacher says that teachers are most affected by inclusion so they should be the ones to decide about it. The third teacher has yet another opinion. "What about the students?" he asks. "Have we ever asked them?"

READER REACTIONS TO "INCLUSION TENSION"

REACTIONS TO "INCLUSION TENSION"

In some ways, the situation at Villa Nueva is not uncommon. On one hand there is a policy that has created significant changes in how schools are organized, and on the other hand there are individuals who will be called upon to implement and live with the policy whether they agreed to it or not. In addition, teachers, like anyone else, can be worried about job security, satisfaction, success, and stress. Underneath these concerns, however, there are sometimes clues indicating bias against disabled students as well as some preference for having them segregated from general education students and teachers. Teachers sometimes think they should have the choice about whether to have special education students in their classrooms, yet who should make such decisions? There is an under-lying belief that one needs a particular expertise to teach disabled students. It would be helpful to consider where that belief comes from. In addition, we find that there is some confusion about whether or not so many Spanish speaking students should be receiving special education services. Over-identification appears to be an issue at Villa Nueva. How do your responses compare to the ones that follow?

Where is the Planning?

Planning is an important aspect of teaching but it is even more crucial for success in inclusive education. Why? Planning for inclusive education requires collaboration between general and special educators, adminis-trators, families, and the larger community. The respondents below indicate their concern about collaboration at all levels of this district.

> I can understand why teachers are somewhat torn about inclusion. I would be too. It looks like this district went into it for one purpose—to increase test scores. There was too little thought to whether or not the risks outweighed the benefits. Didn't anyone consider the research on inclusion? I wonder what that research says. This case makes me worried about how I will react if something like this happens to me.
>
> —A Prospective Teacher and Parent

> It doesn't seem that much thought was given to professional development when the district first started inclusion. There's no evidence of that, anyway. Teachers have a hard job as it is without the introduction of huge changes in their responsibilities. The administration seemed to think that inclusion

would be the answer to low test scores. Why didn't Dr. Flores anticipate the possibility that it wouldn't solve that problem? This can't be the first time a district has tried something like this and then learned it wasn't a cure-all.

—A Teacher

I am concerned about the students with IEPs. Federal law requires us to write IEPs that are individualized. Each child's IEP must meet that particular child's needs. One aspect of these decisions is where services will be provided. Will the individuals involved in planning the IEPs for my students unanimously agree that inclusion is the best option for all students? I can't say that they will. What will happen if parents disagree with inclusion for their child? Does the district have a process in place to communicate the policy with parents and to resolve conflicts when they will inevitably arise? If so, what is it? Were any parents on the ad hoc committee that worked on this policy? I believe in inclusion but I also believe that some children are not prepared to spend all day every day in a general education classroom. I'm not ready to give up individualization. It's still the law, after all. I have seen it work. A couple of the students on my caseload still need resource room support. What will happen to them when they're thrust into general education all day?

—A Special Education Teacher

Defining Inclusion

Dr. Flores indicates that inclusion is consistent with the federal requirement of creating access to the general education curriculum and making yearly progress as a school. It appears that his definition of inclusion is that all students should be in general education full time and receive their support services in general education. However, a previous respondent indicates that a full range of placement options—a continuum of services—is required by law. This is true, but the law also requires access to the general education curriculum. Policy often contains paradoxes like this. This particular paradox raises the question of how to define and practice inclusion. Following are some responses that reveal struggles with these issues.

I'm surprised that all teachers at Villa Nueva don't know what inclusion is. It's not something new. It's been around for at least 25 years. Inclusion is not a part-time thing. To include means to make everyone a full member of the community. Everyone participates on an equal level and everyone belongs. Inclusion doesn't allow segregation. Part-time placement in special education is not inclusion. If it's not clearly defined I think that things might be sloppy and everyone will have their own idea of what inclusion means. I am currently observing in an inclusion classroom. I have been impressed with the way the teacher makes sure every child is participating at his or her level. There is a child with Down Syndrome in this class and if she didn't look different, I'm not sure I would realize she has special needs. The students all treat her like everyone else. She does the same lessons as everyone. Sometimes I notice that the teacher gives her different activities or modified worksheets but a lot of times she expects her to do exactly what other students are doing.

—A Pre-Service Teacher

Inclusion isn't a place where students sit, it's a philosophy, a belief that everyone is welcome and everyone belongs. It means that every adult in the school feels responsible for every student, regardless of the student's race or disability. In an inclusive school, children's needs are met without segregation because inclusive education values diversity. My daughter has autism but when she starts school I want her to be included in kindergarten with her cousin of the same age. I hope my daughter will never be excluded.

—A Mother

Yesterday I was visiting a middle school and the special education teacher introduced me to her "inclusion students." These were students who leave her classroom to attend general education classes several periods a day. We followed a small group of students to their English class. In the classroom, the "included students" sat together and somewhat apart from all the other students. They didn't interact at all. The teacher wasn't welcoming of the "included students" and didn't address them during the period. When they needed assistance, the special education teacher helped them. Strangely, one of the "included" students was seated facing the back wall of the classroom. No one addressed him, not even the other special education students. I asked the special education teacher why he was seated that way and she said, "He knows why. He is missing a lot of assignments and when he catches up, he can join the rest of the class." I couldn't help but wonder why this was being called inclusion when it was really so exclusive.

—A Special Education Teacher Educator

Attitudes Toward Students are Revealing

Teachers' attitudes about disabled students are revealed in some of their comments. Referring to disabled students as "those kids" recalls phrases when racial stereotypes were invoked, consisting of comments about "those people." Viewing disabled students as making things "more complicated" suggests that they are unwelcome problems, yet it speaks to the question of what kind of difference disability makes.

> I was surprised at what the teacher said about students with special needs. What do they mean by "those kids"? Aren't all the kids in the building "their kids"? My child deserves to be in the general education classroom just like everyone else. He shouldn't have to earn his way in and he shouldn't be on probation while there, waiting to get kicked out. Schools can't segregate other children, so how come they can get away with segregating children with special needs? I don't want my child segregated. How is segregating children with special needs any different than segregating African American students? Why doesn't my child deserve access to the same opportunities that everyone else has?
>
> —White Parent of Special Education Student

> The teacher who is worried about having students with such diverse needs is expressing a real concern of teachers. It's hard enough to teach without increasing the diversity of the classroom even more than it already is. For many of us, some kids with disabilities can be the tipping point of what we can handle. In my classroom, I have children who speak ten different languages. Five of my students are English Language Learners and two of those are very recent immigrants to the US. I have five students who receive special education and three of them are reading well below grade level. My class is typical for my school. All the teachers are struggling with how to teach such a diverse group of students. Today's teachers are supposed to do so much with so little, so I can understand why some don't want wholesale inclusion. It makes life more difficult. Some days I go home and feel like such a failure. I know that I didn't accomplish my goals for the day and didn't finish my lesson plans. It's no wonder that 50% of teachers leave the profession in the first five years.
>
> —Elementary Teacher

> I think teachers too often are confused about what is special education and what does it mean to be a student in special education. I think they just view it as being a label, a problem, someone who doesn't want to learn, someone who is hopeless. As a result, they think you have to be some sort of expert to be a special education teacher. My work as a paraprofessional has taught me that special education students are like all other students. The only difference is their labels. In fact, I decided to become a general education teacher because I wanted to be able to include special education students in

my classroom. I think I can help general education teachers understand that good teaching is good teaching and students are students.

—A Pre-Service General Education Teacher and
Special Education Paraprofessional

Changing Professional Roles

Any significant change from "the way things have always been done" can be met with resistance that can last years. When disabled students are segregated in separate classrooms, general and special education teachers work in their own spheres. However, inclusion requires changing professional roles in which general and special educators need to collaborate closely to assure that students' needs are met. Often, this collaboration takes the form of co-teaching. In the following responses, we see that the success of inclusion comes down to the people involved with implementing it. Good intentions are not enough. Systemic reform is necessary to assure the proper support for teachers and students.

I wish the Villa Nueva teachers could visit my school. I co-teach with a special education teacher. At first, I did most of the planning and she came in and helped kids who were having trouble with the work. But over time, we have learned from each other. We started planning together, mostly because I learned that I needed to know how to plan lessons that all my students could benefit from. My co-teacher wanted to feel more confident with the subject matter and wanted a chance to teach some lessons. With time our teaming has been really important to my feelings of success and fulfillment as a teacher. It's sure a lot nicer to have someone else to bounce ideas around. Now, things don't depend on me alone and I feel like I've made a difference in the lives of kids I used to have trouble reaching.

—Sheryl, Middle School Math Teacher, Co-Teaches
with Special Educator

I co-teach with Sheryl. We've been working together for about five years. I asked her if she'd try things out when I transferred to her school and she was willing. So we started the next year, my second year here. At first, my goal was just to make sure my caseload students did well in her class. But after a while, I discovered that her mathematics expertise and my individualization and differentiation expertise together were more successful than either one alone. Once we got comfortable with our arrangement, I noticed that some of my math was coming back to me. I had been a math minor in college. I suggested that we plan together and that we take turns teaching and working

Over-identification

Mrs. Rivera and Dr. Simmons both noticed that too many English Language Learners attending Villa Nueva are being identified for special education services. Over-identification is not limited to Villa Nueva's Hispanic students; it is a nation-wide problem (Losen & Orfield, 2002). The following respondents grapple with this and point out the conundrum of limited resources for support services other than special education.

I empathize with the staff at this school. It is so difficult to know how to meet the needs of students who have not gained English fluency. It can be difficult to assess whether an English language learner is also a student with an impairment. My district has excellent support services, including psychologists who specialize in bilingual assessments. But we are a rich district with no lack of resources. I can't imagine what it's like in districts where they can't afford highly specialized experts.

—A Bilingual Teacher

General education teachers at my school refer a lot of Latino kids to special education. They feel as if they can't do much for those kids who don't speak English that well, and special education is the only way the kids will get attention and support at their level. It's a shame that they have to make them Learning Disabled to get support they need, but the kids' parents don't object as it gets presented to them as extra help. Everyone knows it's not really right, but how else will those kids get that additional support?

—Middle School Counselor

I have been in special education since 1st grade. I was held back in 3rd grade because of reading. I don't know what it would be like to be in general education. My *abuela* doesn't speak English, so I help her when she needs anything. She lives downstairs. My parents also prefer to speak Spanish in the apartment. They work long hours in jobs that don't pay very much money. It is their dream that I go to college, but I am afraid to go because I am not used to work that students do in regular classes. Now I am in 9th grade and I think I will never get out of special education. I might as well drop out.

—Bilingual High School Student

READER REACTIONS

SUMMARY AND ADDITIONAL QUESTIONS

This case demonstrates the complex set of factors that must be anticipated when a school or district implements inclusive education. Some of the factors might be outside the control of teachers, such as whether or not sufficient resources are provided to teachers and schools. Other factors are within the control of teachers. For example, exploring basic beliefs about disability, how beliefs influence attitudes, and in turn, how attitudes influence choices about how to best educate students—show how the power of teacher decisions impact upon the lives of children. It is important to note how being aware of the connection between teacher beliefs and teacher decision-making is the first step of reflective teaching.

Of course, many policies are good and could produce equitable outcomes for students. Teacher and parent responses to equity policies can determine whether or not such policies are going to be effective and have the desired outcomes. In this case, a policy that was intended to be equitable might not be successful because teachers do not appear prepared, specific plans for professional development have not been articulated, negative beliefs about disabled students exist and have not been addressed and dispelled, and the specific support systems are not systematically utilized. These factors are often the very roadblocks that prevent schools from becoming places where all students have equal access to an excellent education.

The case also raises the issue of who should decide about matters of inclusion. The disagreements among respondents mirror the kind of dissent in society at large and the question of who gets to decide is a question that must be examined from the standpoint of all citizens within a democracy. Who gets to decide who's in and who's out? As you contemplate this case, consider what a teacher—perhaps you—could do to counteract roadblocks to equity and uphold the values of democratic education.

Finally, we must ponder the question of what it takes to be an inclusive school. Can any one teacher make inclusion work without the commitment of strong school leadership, supportive administrators and teaching colleagues, paraprofessionals, and families? Furthermore, we should consider the role of students in creating an inclusive school. What kind of intentions and commitments are required from each of these groups if inclusion is to be successful? Further questions to ponder include the following.

1 In this case, there was some confusion about the purposes of inclusion. How would you define "inclusion" and based on your definition, what are its purposes? How would you practice

inclusive education? What supports would you need to be successful?

2   Some of the teachers in this case were worried about how much more complex their job has become with inclusion. Based on the diversity in schools today, is it possible to have full inclusion where all student needs are met in the general education classroom? Why or why not? If so, what might it look like?

3   For prospective teachers, what else do you believe your teacher education program should provide that would help you prepare to work in an inclusive classroom?

4   As a potential or actual teacher, where do you currently draw the line on inclusion? Which students would be "in" the general education classroom and which ones would you say should be "out"? What are your reasons?

5   Equity is an important aspect of democratic education. Many educators say that inclusion promotes equity in education. What kinds of equity might inclusive education provide? How might inclusion create more democratic schools? What challenges for equity or democracy could inclusion pose?

6   Some have said that schools are microcosms of society. In what ways does the debate at Villa Nueva mirror current debates about disabled people in society?

7   One of the hallmarks of democracy is the involvement of its members in making decisions about the way things should be. Regarding inclusion, there is likely to be a good deal of disagreement. Who should make the decision about whether or not to practice inclusive education and why?

8   What do you know about how children with disabilities think and feel about being educated in inclusive classrooms?

9   In many ways, inclusion challenges a "one size fits all" model of teaching. In what ways is equity related to providing differentiated instruction when needed?

10 One of the parents who responded to this case was a White mother of a special education student. She compared segregating disabled students to segregating African American students. There are those who might call the latter racism. Does disability discrimination compare at all to racism and if so, in what way? If not, why not?

INTRODUCTION TO CASE 2

Several teachers and parents at Villa Nueva held attitudes and beliefs about disability that originated from somewhere. Perhaps it was personal experience. Perhaps they had concerns about the unknown. Or maybe they had heard stories from other teachers. Yet, their beliefs persisted even when Jennifer and Sandy disagreed and contradicted them with evidence of their own experience. This indicates how strong our assumptions can be, even when evidence may directly disprove them.

Bias against disabled people in general is fairly common. As with other forms of bias, ableism is associated with people's unacknowledged expectation of how they think all bodies should look and function. Societal expectations of all citizens in regard to health, physical and emotional milestones, intellectual abilities, beauty, "appropriate" social interactions, and so on, can result in discriminatory actions against those viewed as disabled. In brief, those who are considered abnormal in physical, cognitive, emotional, or behavioral ways—experience life very differently than non-disabled people.

In Case 2, we find that ableism is difficult to recognize in oneself until it is revealed in some meaningful way. Unfortunately, unrecognized or tacit ableism can drive teacher decisions in ways that are harmful to students. In this case, we see that ableism harms all students in the classroom to one degree or another. Sometimes, ableism is both invisible and pervasive, as it seems to be for one of the teachers in this case study. As you follow the case you will see how teacher beliefs and daily decisions teachers make based on their beliefs shape curriculum opportunities for students. What are your current beliefs about disability and how might they affect your teaching?

CASE 2: "ABLEISM AT FOREST RUN ELEMENTARY"

"He's a flatliner," states Shelly Mitchell, a special education teacher at Forest Run Elementary School. "He functions at a low level—and there's no movement!" Judith Sheldon overhears Shelly matter-of-factly telling the school psychologist what she thinks about Jesse, the 2nd grader the psychologist is getting ready to evaluate for special education services. Even though Shelly's comment seems insensitive to Judith, Jesse's 2nd grade teacher, she knows that Shelly cares about students and wants them to succeed. They co-teach together every day and Judith has seen Shelly's commitment to students, including Jesse. This is why Shelly's comments seem so paradoxical to Judith.

"Sometimes," thinks Judith, "Shelly says things that she might regret if she really thought about them. I'm also concerned about Jesse's achievement levels, but I wouldn't call him a *flatliner*."

Judith is very familiar with the way Shelly describes Jesse, a youngster who transferred to suburban Forest Run from another district at the end of the last school year. When Jesse arrived, his literacy was assessed at a pre-kindergarten level and he was referred to the building child study team to determine whether interventions were necessary. The child study team implemented some interventions that included Reading Recovery. Since then, he has made progress relative to where he started less than six months ago. He's now reading at a 1st grade level, yet Shelly has been persistent in pressing for him to be evaluated for special education eligibility even though Jesse is quite young at this time. Since the beginning of the year, she has talked about his "blank expression" and "dull eyes." During the first week of school, she recommended that Judith place him in the lowest reading group, and since then, has frequently expressed concern about his lack of achievement.

Shelly's statement triggers a memory of a situation in Judith's previous school, where the student population was primarily African American and Hispanic. There, a 4th grade teacher would thoroughly read every student's complete school file prior to the school year. She would prepare reading and math groups based on what she read in the files, even before the students entered her classroom. Judith observed that these students always remained in the same group throughout the entire year. There was no movement to another group based on student performance or the teacher's deepened understanding of the students.

Even as a student teacher, Judith experienced a similar encounter with a teacher in a wealthy suburban school. She was visiting a teacher's classroom prior to being placed for student teaching. As she knocked on the door, the teacher greeted her and stood in the doorway, pointing to a youngster in the front row near the door. "He doesn't belong in this room. He just moved here from Detroit," she said. "He belongs in the special education room. I'm trying to get the special education teacher to keep him full time." Judith remembers her heart sinking as she realized that the teacher was talking loudly enough for the whole class to hear. For a while, Judith considered becoming a special education teacher, but she eventually decided to stick with general education.

Judith's attention is pulled back to the present as she hears Shelly's door close and the recess bell ring. It's Judith's prep period and as she closes her door, the psychologist, Mr. Jeffreys, walks in behind her and asks, "As his teacher, what are your thoughts about Jesse?"

"I'm perplexed," answers Judith. "I know that he is reading below grade level, but he has made a good deal of progress. I also know that we can't predict whether he'll continue to make enough progress to catch up with his peers. If he doesn't, this might be the critical time to intervene."

"How much do you think his physical appearance has to do with Shelly's insistence that he be evaluated?" asks Mr. Jeffreys.

This question and her conversation with Mr. Jeffreys gives Judith an idea. Since she co-teaches with Shelly, Judith decides to invite Shelly to co-plan a language arts unit on difference. The next day, when Judith presents the idea, Shelly agrees.

"This would also fit with our current science unit on the categories of living organisms, since this week we're studying organisms that have backbones," mentions Shelly.

"Differences between organisms sounds like a concept somewhat related to differences between people," responds Judith. "I'm thinking about making direct links to the ways in which people treat others who are different and the consequences of that. So, I'm hoping we can make connections to social values rather than just natural variation."

"Oh, I see. That sounds more like something related to what we're doing in social studies right now," suggests Shelly.

Judith nods and continues, "I was just reading a very old Japanese folk-tale called *Crow Boy* by Taro Yashima. It's about Chibi, a boy who is teased by the other children in school because they think he's slow. He comes to school dressed in ragged clothes, with little to eat, and the children know that he is from a poor family. One day the children learn that he can make the sounds of birds and when they learn about his talent, they regret tormenting him. I thought we might start with that story." Judith wonders if Shelly will make the connection between the story and her opinions about Jesse.

As the women plan the unit, they expand their ideas to include concepts related to difference. "I once heard that *The Little Mermaid* story reflects negative attitudes about disability," suggests Shelly one day during a planning session.

"That's new to me," responds Judith. "What are the negative attitudes?"

"The mermaid wanted to walk so she could marry her prince. She was unable to walk," says Shelly. "Does that give girls the impression that they will only be acceptable if they walk or if their bodies are perfect?"

"I wonder what else we could use from children's popular culture to emphasize these ideas?" asks Judith.

"What about using other folktales?" adds Shelly.

"Oh, yes, *Beauty and the Beast*," says Judith and then she lists other literature selections in the district's language arts curriculum guide: *The Ugly Duckling, Mufaro's Beautiful Daughters*. "These all contain messages about the social value of beauty."

The next day, Mr. Jeffreys returns to see Jesse for the evaluation and finds him in Shelly's resource room visiting with some other children. When Mr. Jeffreys entered the room, Shelly had been thinking about her description of Jesse as a "flatliner." As Jesse leaves with Mr. Jeffreys, Shelly's face turns bright red when suddenly remembering her "flatliner" comments yesterday and realizing that like Chibi in *Crow Boy*, Shelly had been making assumptions about Jesse's abilities based on his appearance and her biases about his background.

The next week, Judith and Shelly teach their first lesson in the new unit. Judith has asked Shelly to begin by reading *Crow Boy* to the students. Then she asks, "Why do you think the children tease Chibi?"

Students have several ideas.

"Because he is slow."

"He can't read."

"He dresses funny."

"They don't like him."

Shelly asks, "Why don't they like him?"

"Because he doesn't live in the village where they live."

"Maybe he smells bad."

Finally, one student says, "He's different than everybody else."

"Why would they tease him if he's different?" asks Shelly.

There are no responses for a while and then Jesse says, "Because people don't like him 'cuz he's different."

Rather than directly asking students how they treat people who are different, Judith and Shelly offer crayons and paper to the students and ask them to draw and write a story like *Crow Boy* but set in their town and at their school. They view this activity as a way for them to assess how their students are thinking about difference. Later, the teachers review what children have done and are surprised by the variety of responses. Both teachers are taken aback by Jesse's drawing and the caption that goes with it. The drawing is of a boy swinging alone on a swing set, a frown on his face. Several other children are standing nearby, pointing at the boy and one of them is saying, "You dummy." Shelly's face burns red hot as she realizes that this depicts a scene similar to her interaction the day before with Mr. Jeffreys. Judith notices Shelly's embarrassment and waits for Shelly to talk first. Finally, Shelly says, "I wonder if this has really happened to Jesse at some point."

"It might have," responds Judith. "Since almost the day he arrived, Jesse has been viewed as different by his teachers and his peers. I believe that has influenced how Jesse is treated as well as how he has performed academically."

"Some differences aren't as subjective as appearances, though," defends Shelly. "For example, Jesse really does test below grade level in reading and math. There's no disputing that."

An additional set of illustrations comes from a small group of children who decided to create a story together. This group of boys is comprised of students who have teased Jesse in the past. One scene in their story depicts three boys—looking very much like the illustrators—surrounding a fourth boy on the playground. One boy is saying to the child in the middle, "Hey stupid." Given the similarities, Judith and Shelly are persuaded that Jesse's scene and this one depict the same incident.

Later that morning, Shelly and Judith share their lesson and the student drawings with other teachers and they are surprised at the variety of interpretations expressed by their colleagues. Most teachers agree that Jesse's peers need to be tolerant of his differences. Judith notices that several teachers share Shelly's view that Jesse's achievement is unrelated to his social experiences and the fact that he comes from a district known for a curriculum less rigorous than Forest Run's curriculum. One teacher remarks that "most students who come from that district are below grade level and they don't often catch up. It's just a fact." As the conversation comes to a close and it's time for bus duty, Judith is anxious to find out what Shelly thinks about everything and hopes they have a chance to talk the next day.

READER REACTIONS TO "ABLEISM AT FOREST RUN ELEMENTARY"

REACTIONS TO "ABLEISM AT FOREST RUN ELEMENTARY"

Ableism is a relatively new term. Thomas Hehir (2002) defines it as "the devaluation of disability" that

> results in societal attitudes that uncritically assert that it is better for people to walk than roll, speak than sign, read print than read Braille, spell independently than use a spell-check, and hang out with nondisabled students as opposed to other disabled students (p. 7).

We could also add that while ableism *devalues* the way some people learn or speak, or look, or move it conversely *values* those considered "normal." In this case, it is unclear whether Jesse is disabled but Shelly's reference to him as a "flatliner" is an ableist remark. It is spoken like an epithet and denigrates people who learn slowly or with difficulty.

It is easy to point a finger at Shelly, but it is useful to remember that ableism does not exist in a vacuum. In *The End of Education*, Neil Postman (1995) writes, "Public education does not serve a public, but creates a public." We could add that school not only creates a public, it also mirrors a public. What we see in this case is what is seen in society at large. We might also consider that Shelly's assumptions about Jesse are the result of her enculturation which is a process of socialization into the set of values and norms to which her community adheres. In Shelly's case, as with many people in the US, social values about ability and assumptions about the meaning behind facial expressions are implied. She might not even realize her values and assumptions. This is where reflective teaching comes in. Everyone is *enculturated*—shaped by the values and social norms of the culture they inhabit. So, a question you might ask yourself is: "What are the values and social norms about ability into which I have been enculturated?"

School as a Microcosm of Society

If schools create a public by preparing young people for a civic life in which they will contribute to the shaping of society, then we must consider the relationship between school, community, and the broader society. The first respondent does this.

> Where does discrimination against people with disabilities come from? An ethnic joke, racial slurs, demeaning language seems to be very common in

today's culture. All kids bring these things to school and by high school they pervade the whole climate. Last year, we stopped segregating students in separate classrooms and went to full inclusion. This was a huge risk for me and the entire school. I knew that if it didn't work and there were crises, my job would be at stake. We've made our mistakes and we're still trying to figure out how to make this succeed to the fullest, but working on including students with disabilities into general education classes has affected my whole school community. I've been surprised that most people have done their part, including parents. Of course many people were cautious or resistant at first, but as a result we have stretched our views of what is possible, and of what our roles are as students, teachers, administrators, and parents to make this work. I know that it has affected how we all think, talk, and act and our change has reached out into the community through media reports and our search for community resources to support our initiative.

—High School Principal

Teacher Assumptions and Student Achievement

The next respondents take varying positions on the relationship between teacher assumptions and student achievement. Some respondents view Shelly's perspective as preventing Jesse from achieving, particularly when it comes to her assumptions about the relationship between his appearance and his academic ability. One respondent wonders how teachers are supposed to make decisions about students without forming some assumptions.

An environment of assumption has been created around Jesse. His teacher continues making whatever assumptions she would like because she assumes that it has no effect on her academic judgment of him. I believe that his achievements will always be in the shadow of his weaknesses and evaluated in relationship to them. Jesse's performance should warrant a boost in the teacher's challenging him to raise his progress to the level that will allow him to continue learning with his peers. Yet she puts him in the lowest groups and expected him to do far less.

—A Prospective Special Education Teacher

Once Shelly makes her assumptions, it will be nearly impossible for Jesse to move beyond them and have a chance of achieving parity with his peers. Another way to say this is that Shelly's assumptions will likely come into fruition, like a self-fulfilling prophecy for Jesse. When I read this I can see Shelly's mistakes but it also makes me think about my own assumptions. Which students do I underestimate? What signals do I send them that convey my view of their inability? How am I part of the problem?

—General Education Teacher

This case shows the dangers involved when one looks only at outside factors like facial expressions and student hygiene to judge others. How do a "blank expression" and "dull eyes" tell anything about a child's academic abilities? Teachers bear the responsibility to help all students succeed according to their needs and abilities, yet Shelly's practice of using looks to make assumptions about children can be potentially dangerous. If only all teachers could work with someone like Judith, who understands and embraces the need for differences, our educational system would be a more welcoming place for all students. I hope that when I am a new teacher I will have someone like Judith to lean upon and learn from. My own child's teacher seems to be that kind of person. Shelly's view of Jesse reminds me of the idea of the "least dangerous assumption." As the parent of a child with autism, I've been trying to practice using the least dangerous assumption about my son. For example, when he doesn't seem to be paying attention, I assume he is and continue talking to him like I would any other person. So far, he has surprised me with how much he takes in under these circumstances.

—Parent of General Education Student and a Pre-Service Teacher

I'm disturbed by the fact that Shelly dismisses Jesse's picture at the end of the case by saying, "Some differences aren't as subjective as appearances." First of all, she has used Jesse's appearances against him. She then goes on to point out that Jesse tests lower than the other children. I think this shows that she is unable or unwilling to consider possible reasons for his test performance. For example, does she know if he has had the same opportunities that other students have had? How many schools has he attended in three short years? Does she know whether his learning difficulties make tests unreliable for assessing his achievement? Finally, why can't she recognize what he *has* achieved?

—Teacher Educator and Parent of Three Elementary Students

I understand why Shelly's view of Jesse is a problem for her teaching and for Jesse's learning. I don't understand how teachers are supposed to work with students without making assumptions about student abilities. Don't we all make assumptions about others? How can a teacher set aside her personal opinions? It seems impossible. In my student teaching assignment I have

tried to be aware of the assumptions I form about my students. I have also
tried to avoid making assumptions but I have found this to be impossible. I
asked my student teaching supervisor about this and she suggested I think
of assumptions as non-judgmental guesses about students that need to be
refined as I continue getting to know students in more depth. She told me
to write down my assumptions and revise them as they change based on
evidence. I'm going to try this.

—Pre-service Special Educator

What Counts as Evidence

What *does* count as evidence of student learning? Shelly's reliance on
standardized test results represents one position in the debate over this
question. Several respondents below have concerns about the evidence
Shelly uses to form her opinions about students. Some respondents see
problems with standardized testing and relying too heavily on test results.
But the next respondent points out the necessity of standardized testing,
noting that most teachers have no choice—testing is a requirement
for most of today's teachers and students. Others find Shelly's reference
to Jesse's physical appearance to be a serious problem and one relates
personally to Jesse's stigma.

While I understand that test results are only one way of assessing
students, most teachers are required to test students. Today, it seems like
schools are either preparing for tests or giving tests. Politicians and
many parents think tests are the best way to measure progress. How
can teachers avoid standardized testing? It's not like I can say, "No
thanks, I'd rather not." If I'm told to test students, I'm going to test them.
If I'm told to spend time preparing them for the test, I'm going to do
it. Without tenure, what choice do I have? With tenure, what choice do
I have?

—Pre-service General Education Teacher

Shelly's use of test scores is interesting. I've learned that test scores are
easy to use and easy to misuse. Considering how much debate there is about
how fair—or unfair—standardized testing is, it is likely that Jesse would
have a tough time taking such a test. After all, he recently moved into this
school from another district where the curriculum was not as rigorous. It
makes sense that Jesse's teacher should take his test results with a grain
of salt. I'm not sure why Shelly ignores other evidence, like his recent
growth in reading. Even though he isn't up to grade level, he has improved

a lot in a short amount of time. She might find authentic assessment a more meaningful tool for determining whether Jesse has learned and what he has learned.

—Pre-service Special Education Teacher

Shelly seems to be drawing conclusions about Jesse based on poor evidence. She describes his achievement not by how far he has come, but rather on the fact that he is still below the level that he "should" be at. Instead of focusing on his success—that he started at a below-kindergarten level and less than six months later is at a 1st grade reading level—she is dwelling on the fact that he is not yet at a 2nd grade reading level. Even typically developing children learn at different rates.

—2nd Grade Teacher

Shelly's strong belief in the integrity and validity of test scores is evident. She appears to be assured that a student's test scores are an accurate reflection of that student's intelligence, skills and competencies. This is all very black and white for Shelly. She is not cognizant of the shades of grey that exist in the real world. She needs to consider the varying student learning styles, myriad test-taking strategies and ways to present information and ask questions that the student may need to adjust to, particularly if things were different in his former district. However, Shelly's understanding is that any result outside the "normal" range indicates a disability, and this does not buy Jesse the additional time he needs to further develop his skills. In my job as a counselor, I often help students who have transferred in to adjust to our school. Some children struggle with that adjustment, particularly if the reason for their move is related to a divorce or some other family crisis. I can't always share the details with teachers, but I try to communicate the importance of giving kids the benefit of the doubt, particularly when they're in transition.

—Elementary School Counselor

Shelly's conclusions about Jesse appear to be based upon her preconceived notions, or "tacit assumptions," far more than his actual talents and abilities. In fact, I would go so far as to say that these ableist notions subconsciously shape her ideas about evidence. For example, she seems to be thinking, "Since Jesse isn't reading at grade level he is either lazy and there is little hope for success, or he needs special education and should be tested." Instead she should be thinking, "Jesse has made progress and gained ground in his reading in six months and that's a good sign." She disregards the second possibility—that Jesse's progress in six short months is an important

factor—because of her assumptions about evidence and her biases against
Jesse's appearance.

—Special Education Teacher

Shelly's poor use of evidence of Jesse's learning is actually disabling him.
Her behavior is a perfect example of ableism. She is creating barriers to his
learning by limiting him and constructing an idea of him as a failure.
Apparently she doesn't realize that this actually impacts her decisions and
his learning. Jesse's drawing at the end is telling as are the reactions of the
other teachers. Their description of the district Jesse came from is worri-
some because it suggests that any student who transfers from that district
will automatically be categorized as Jesse was. What evidence do they have
about the other district and why do they generalize like they do? I teach in
a district where student achievement tests scores are lower than the
surrounding district. I suspect that students transferring from my district to
a nearby district probably get the same treatment that Jesse has received. It's
discouraging since I believe that the teachers in my district work extremely
hard to help kids achieve. We sometimes seem to be fighting a losing battle,
though, especially since we have moved to an emphasis on authentic assessment. This means that we try to determine if students have learned by
observing their overall performance, noting how they engage in learning
activities and the work that they produce. This puts us at a bit of a disadvantage when trying to communicate student learning to others, particularly
those in districts where the emphasis is on standardized tests. Sometimes
I'm embarrassed to tell someone where I teach because I worry that I'll be
labeled just like the students in the district are labeled.

—An 8th Grade Teacher

I can relate to Jesse's situation. I have cerebral palsy and people make
assumptions about me all the time based on my physical appearance.
Because it's difficult for me to talk, people assume I can't understand them
and they raise their voice and talk both slower and louder, as though I'm
cognitively impaired and deaf. When they figure out that I'm neither and I
understand what they're saying, they still assume I can't speak for myself
and seem impatient or uncomfortable when I am talking. If I'm in a
restaurant or anywhere in public, people will talk to my attendant and ignore
me. Fortunately, I have personal assistants who direct the conversation to
me. But it's frustrating that this happens all the time and that in the twenty-
first century people still have these misconceptions about cerebral palsy. It's
not just people with cerebral palsy, either. I have a close friend, Charlie,
who has Aspergers. That's kind of like autism. Charlie can talk, he's really
smart—an engineer. But he has trouble socializing and because of some

unusual behaviors . . . people tend to avoid him, so he has always been a loner. When we were kids, Charlie was teased mercilessly in school. Teachers sort of ignored him in class as though he wasn't worth paying attention to. I'm sad to say that Charlie was treated like a freak because he didn't know how to connect with people, plus he had some unusual tics. Our teachers underestimated him almost as much as they underestimated me.

—A Parent

The Curriculum

The "hidden curriculum" (sometimes referred to as the "unofficial curriculum") in Shelly's classroom is very likely teaching students about who counts and who does not. It is clear that Jesse does not seem to count in Shelly's hidden curriculum, or the unintentional, unplanned, serendipitous messages students are exposed to. The first respondent speaks to the issue of the hidden curriculum. On the other hand, when teachers select materials and activities that intentionally and explicitly provide opportunities to explore, understand, and reflect upon difference, the curriculum can help children de-mystify disability or any difference. Judith uses children's literature to do this, while also considering her teaching partner, Shelly, whose reference to Jesse as a "flatliner" was too disturbing to ignore.

This case study was an eye opener for me. It made me realize that situations like this go on all the time, unfortunately even in my own building. I am sure that students in Shelly's classroom know what she thinks about Jesse. She blatantly throws around her opinion about him as a flatliner. It's kind of like something that happened this afternoon when I was helping my students get on the bus to go home. My students ride a special education bus. Today, the bus driver was a substitute. As I walked up to the bus with two of my students she asked, "How many wheelchairs do you have?" At first I didn't know what she meant. I don't have any wheelchairs. Then I realized that right there in front of my two students, she was referring to students like them who are wheelchair users! This sort of thing is not uncommon. In fact, a similar thing happened to me yesterday. One of my new students has Down Syndrome. Another special education teacher saw me in the hall and asked, "How is your new Downs?" My students were nearby and I'm sure they heard this. All I could think of was, "Why would you refer to her as a 'Downs'?" She's a girl. Her name is Adrian. She is a good reader who loves to jump rope. She is not a "Downs." If I taught general education he would probably ask, "How is the new student?" or "How is the new girl?" or "How is Adrian settling in?" These comments about wheelchairs and "Downs"

may seem meaningless to many people, but to me these words and interactions teach children as effectively as any lesson in a classroom. They
teach children who others think their peers are. So: Jesse is a "flatliner"
instead of a boy who has made good progress in reading; my students
getting on the bus are "wheelchairs" instead of two boys who are best
friends heading to a sleepover; and, my new student is a "Downs" instead
of a girl with a name who likes to read.

—A Special Education Teacher

I'm impressed with Judith's ability to sensitively guide Shelly toward
thinking about difference by using children's literature and the curriculum.
I'm even more impressed that it's a general education teacher doing this
with a special education teacher. I would have expected it to be the other
way around—so this is a welcome debunk of my own stereotypes! Literature
has long been used as a way to teach lessons and enlighten readers. In my
job, I often choose books that speak to particular social issues when I'm
holding book talks or reading circles. I have used *Crow Boy* before but in a
slightly different context. In fact, I find it quite effective to focus on folktales from around the world. They tend to make values or biases visible and
children seem to be drawn to them.

—Parent and Children's Librarian

Ableism Affects Everyone

In the case, a group of boys illustrate a scene similar to the one Jesse has
illustrated. The teachers are convinced that the two scenes represent a very
real experience. This is an example of the influence of ableism on all
students—disabled and non-disabled, students, parents, and teachers.
Discrimination and bias can permeate the social atmosphere in school and
when modeled and/or tolerated by teachers it can infect interpersonal
relationships.

It was difficult for me to read this case because it reminds me of a difficult
experience when my youngest son was in elementary school. A similar situation happened to him. When he was in 3rd grade we moved to a new school,
and very soon his teacher was calling me to say she was sure he was learning
disabled. My husband and I didn't want him tested at first. We thought
maybe he was having trouble adjusting but we knew that he had difficulty
in his previous school. Nonetheless, his teacher was convinced that he
should be tested for special education. She pressured us by sending notes
home everyday outlining what he didn't do that day. When he didn't finish

his homework, she would keep him in from recess to complete it. She even went so far as to tell him that if we would just test him for special education, he could get the help he needed. One day, I was in the school office and I overheard her talking in the hall outside the door. She was telling another teacher that we had refused testing and that she was "tired of bending over backwards to help a slow kid when his parents were in denial and won't even help." The teacher said she had other students who deserved her help since their parents were supportive. I was so upset, I wanted to cry. I had to leave without staying to volunteer in the library. Thinking about that now, I believe that her ableism was in the way because she thought other students were more deserving of her help. Since our son was slow, and we hadn't done what she wanted us to do, she thought we were being negligent in some way, and our son was Learning Disabled.

—A Mother

This case shows how ableism affects everyone, not just people who have disabilities. I recently subbed for a special education teacher at a middle school because she had to attend meetings. I was supposed to escort her students to their "inclusion" classrooms. I was told that these students had learning disabilities or emotional and behavioral disorders. Each period, I would walk three or four of her students to a different class—English, science, math. In every class, the special education students entered and no one greeted them. The teachers didn't say hello. The other students didn't even look at them. The special education students tended to sit at the back of each classroom, separated physically from the other students and far from where the teachers stood. In the English class, one of the special education students—Dejuan—sat separated even from the other special education students. He just stared at the wall the entire class. In science, the special education students worked individually on science projects but the general education students were working on projects in small groups. Again, the two sets of students never interacted. At the end of the day, I asked the special education teacher, "Why are your students excluded?" She seemed startled by this question but I thought I had interpreted the situation accurately. I specifically asked her about Dejuan, who seemed so isolated and disconnected. She said, "He chooses to be there. He doesn't want to interact with anybody." To tell you the truth, I didn't really feel good after subbing in that school.

—A Pre-service General Education Teacher

I like to sit alone. I am labeled emotionally disturbed. I am a good reader, and saw this when my homeroom teacher left my files around in class. I don't give a shit about what people think of me. I have made it to 8th grade, but hate school. It's sooooooooooooooo boring. The stuff we learn about has nothing to do with my life. I am living with my aunt, but can tell she doesn't really want me there. She already has three kids. My bedroom is next to hers. Sometimes I hear her crying at night after she's argued with my uncle. She thinks he's going to leave. My mother died two years ago, so my aunt and uncle took me in because they didn't want me to go into foster care. But now they're having problems of their own. I have an eye disease that makes it difficult to see sometimes, and I have been told to wear glasses—but don't want to look like a nerd. The teachers are doing their job, but don't really care if I'm here or not. I hate school. I am tired of everything.

—Dejuan, 8th Grade Student Labeled Emotionally Disturbed

I see this group of kids coming into my classroom with another teacher. It makes me feel uncomfortable because I think how much I wouldn't want to be in their position. I mean everyone knows that they're the sped kids. My mom wasn't very happy when she heard I was in one of those inclusion classes, so she came to see the principal. But he said there weren't that many sped kids in my class, and it wouldn't make a difference about what I was learning. There's a girl who's in that sped group that I'd like to talk to, but I'd feel weird because my friends would probably tease me, and call me a retard.

—Gabriel, 8th Grade General Education Student

READER REACTIONS

SUMMARY AND ADDITIONAL QUESTIONS

As stated earlier, Shelly's ableism cannot be viewed in a vacuum, free of its social environment. Ableism, racism, or any set of discriminatory beliefs and practices must be understood within a broader context. In the preface, we used the metaphor of a landscape and the lenses used to view it. First, think of the contexts in which ableism is generally found across the educational landscape. Next, zoom in and we see a small portion of the landscape or specific examples like the one in this case—a student is described as a flatliner by an authority figure, a general education student afraid of associating with an included student in case of being thought of as "a retard." Draw back, and once again consider the whole landscape and how this case fits within the broader society. Consider the ways in which society creates schools. For example, ableism has long permeated society in terms of creating and circulating stereotypes. Remember Tiny Tim in the story of *A Christmas Carol* and the way other characters pitied him? Do characters like Tiny Tim emerge solely from the imagination of writers or from the absorption of social values? Or think about descriptions of disabled people "overcoming great odds"— a figure known as the "super-crip" to many in the disability community. Reflect on how often the media sensationalizes an amputee who climbs Mount Everest or goes sky diving, a deaf person who is a professional musician, or a wheelchair user who dances, as though it is unusual for the disabled to have talents or simply to do what others do.

The last respondents to this case illustrate how ableism's effects are not isolated to disabled people. It affects the whole environment. At Forest Run, both colleagues and students were affected by Shelly's negative attitude toward Jesse. Such ableist messages within the environment influence behavior toward others, including Jesse. The curriculum was constrained by Shelly's low expectations of Jesse (and perhaps other students). Some might argue that the curriculum was constrained by Shelly's over-emphasis, perhaps even a reliance, upon standardized test results, although of course today's teachers are relentlessly pressured to think in these ways. Based on what respondents said, we could assume that Jesse's parents and perhaps likely other parents in the school are affected by the ableism at the core of this case.

The last respondent vividly describes the way ableism can affect everyone. If the respondent felt discouraged after subbing at the school, can you imagine how the special education students feel every day? Think about the effect that isolation of one's peers has on the development of the general education students. What are they learning about our society by being in classes that segregate and isolate other students? The general education teachers are not unaffected, either. Can it be possible for them to feel good about what they are doing? If it is possible, what does that say about them as individuals, or teaching as a profession? Ableism is a whole-school, whole-community, whole-society affair. As you reflect on this case, consider the following questions.

1   Four disability stereotypes are mentioned above: widespread versions of people with disabilities such as Tiny Tims and super-crips; Shelly's caricature of Jesse as a flatliner; the omnipresent fear of "contagion" if too near a person with a disability ("retard" by approximation). What other disability stereotypes can you think of? What are some examples of these stereotypes in your everyday life? In what other ways are people with disabilities stereotyped?

2   Stereotypes pervade the social atmosphere and most of us believe them—at least to some degree—without recognizing it. In what ways have you stereotyped disabled people?

3   Whether or not Shelly had openly discussed her opinion about Jesse's abilities, it is likely that Jesse would have a sense of what she thought of him. In what ways do teachers transmit their opinion of students (words, actions, body language, expecta-tions) without coming right out and saying what they think? How can a teacher's opinion influence how young students assess themselves?

4   In this case, Shelly's position on what counts as evidence has worked against Jesse because she has a narrow view of what counts. In what ways can "evidence" be used to disable students? In what ways can it be used to enable students?

5   What do you consider good evidence of whether or not a student is disabled? What is your role as a teacher in making that decision?

6   If you had been in the same position as Judith, how might you have reacted to Shelly's characterization of Jesse? In many ways, Judith's approach was indirect—assuming that Shelley would make associations between the story and Jesse. Is an indirect approach better to a direct approach of addressing the issues? If so, why? If not, why not? What might a direct approach have sounded like?

7   In what ways is ableism a fitting way to contemplate everyday situations, both in school and out, about disability?

INTRODUCTION TO CASE 3

In today's political climate of high stakes testing and federal threats to withhold funding if schools cannot increase student achievement, under-resourced schools struggle to find solutions to the challenges facing their students. Schools sometimes call upon the surrounding community to consider the nature and source of the problems and potential solutions. The solutions to complex problems facing such schools often depend upon the perspective of the ones offering those solutions, as well as those who have the power to make decisions that stick.

Case 3 looks at the problems and debates at Central Valley High School (CVHS), which is a school facing serious financial and academic decline while under pressure to increase achievement with fewer and fewer resources. While everyone involved attributes the decline, in part, to reduced funding, there is an undercurrent suggesting other reasons for the decline, as well. When the entire community, including the media, gets involved, numerous solutions are posed and issues are raised that suggest a relationship between race, class, and disability. At the heart of this case are several interrelated questions: from where should low achieving poor African American and Hispanic students get the academic support they need? On a larger scale: why are so many poor African American and Hispanic students failing academically? And finally, perhaps most import-antly, how does racism disable students?

CASE 3: "RACE, PLACE, AND THE SEARCH FOR SOLUTIONS"

For as long as anyone can remember, CVHS, a multi-ethnic urban school, has been on the district and state "watch list" of schools that are failing due to low student achievement on high stakes standardized tests.

Resources are limited in the district. Due to lack of funds, the building is run down. Students sit in classrooms that are chilly in winter and stifling hot in summer. They use textbooks that are sorely outdated and since there aren't enough textbooks for everyone, no one can take them home to study. There is only one computer lab with outdated equipment, machines that are slow to run, and intermittent Internet access. There are few extra-curricular options for students and of those they have, there are no aca-demically oriented options like science club or debate team.

Veteran Central Valley faculty members recall a time when they were able to provide counseling and after school programs for students "at risk" for school failure, which they claim includes almost the entire student body today. In those days, extra-curricular activities included sports for boys and girls; a debate team; chess, science, and math clubs; a book club; an honor society; and much more. Although textbooks were in short supply then, as now, teachers had enough extras that the students who really wanted to take a book home could do so if it was brought back the next day.

In faculty meetings, teachers express frustration over the lack of funding for current textbooks and basic technology, after school activities, field trips, and support personnel like social workers and psychologists. In addition to the lack of resources, all schools in Central Valley district feel the pressure of federal mandates that, if not achieved, will result in withdrawal of crucial funding.

CVHS is quite typical of urban, multi-ethnic schools today. The student body is 75% African American, 20% Hispanic (many of whom are English Language Learners), 3% Euro-American, and 2% Asian, most of whom recently immigrated to the US. Typical of many schools like CVHS, 98% of the students qualify for free lunch and 99% live below the poverty line. Only 60% of the school's Hispanic students and 55% of the African American students graduate. The graduation rate for the Euro-American and Asian students is significantly higher (85%) but still too low.

In addition, and again like other urban schools, CVHS has a large special education population. A total of 18% of its students are eligible for special education; a high percentage compared to the national average. Of the special education students, 85% are African American and 13% are Hispanic English Language Learners.

Central High's principal, Dr. Watkins, is one of the first African American administrators in the district. She does what she can to raise money for after school tutoring programs and other support services but there is only so much that can be done in today's political climate in which the media and community organizations describe the district's schools as "failing our children." The local African American newspaper has been particularly vocal about the district's apparent inability to create what it calls a "climate of achievement" for African American students.

In a faculty meeting, Dr. Watkins begins by announcing, "It's time we stop worrying about what other people have to say about our work. We need to know what we think about our work."

She then asks teachers to identify and prioritize a list of their greatest concerns about their student body. Teachers generate a long list of concerns and when prioritized, the top five priorities are:

1   classroom management

2   pressures of standardized testing

3   lack of resources

4   student apathy

5   tensions between school and broader community.

To everyone's surprise, Dr. Watkins then reveals that she asked the parents attending the previous night's Parent Organization meeting to do the same activity. She displays their top five priorities on an overhead projector:

1   the school's watch list status based on state achievement test results

2   classroom management

3   lack of support services

4   teacher apathy

5   unresponsiveness of the school to community concerns.

Rumbling is heard throughout the meeting room. Teachers wonder what Dr. Watkins plans to do with this information. Signithia Randall, the building's newest science teacher, is heard saying, "We clearly have some work to do."

After debating their next steps, the faculty and Dr. Watkins agree that a general meeting with the school faculty, the school administration, and the Parent Organization is needed.

At the meeting two weeks later, Dr. Watkins stands before the entire audience and displays the two prioritized lists of concerns.

"What are we going to do about these issues?" she asks the gathering.

Hands go up and one by one she calls on people to offer their ideas.

Parent suggestions include "Have after school tutoring every night of the week instead of once a week," and "Do a better job of preparing students for the state tests," and "Hire more African American teachers." This last suggestion was based on a common complaint about the Central District teaching force, which is mostly White.

Some teachers also share ideas such as "Have a building-wide classroom management system," and "Increase the number of special education faculty to provide services for the students who need help but aren't getting it."

In response to this last suggestion, several parents and community members begin talking all at once. Some of them are supportive.

"If more students could get individual instruction, it would help. Why not make sure the special education department is seeing as many students as possible?"

And, "Yeah, there's lots of money for special education and too little money for regular education."

One parent adds, "My son is in special education and he's making A's and B's now."

Others disagree, saying, "Special education isn't the answer. It wouldn't improve instruction in the regular classes."

"It wouldn't raise test scores," adds another parent.

One voice calls out, "I was in special education and I didn't even graduate. I don't want that for my children."

Still another says, "I don't understand why the Spanish speaking students always get put in special education."

"Why don't the teachers just teach? When I was in school, you listened and teachers taught all period every period, every day," added another.

Sitting in the back of the auditorium, Signithia isn't sure where she stands on these issues but she is sure that something definitely needs to be done. She turns to her mentor, the Science Department Chair, and says, "How can I prepare students for graduation, much less college? My science lab was built when the school was opened fifty years ago. The faucets don't work so I can't run water. The chemistry supplies are at least twenty to thirty years old and I don't have a key to the cabinet in which they're locked."

"You wouldn't want to use those chemicals, anyway, would you?" asks her Department Chair.

"No. And my chemistry textbooks are so outdated, the latest scientific discoveries aren't even in them! I can't believe I still don't have a computer in my classroom."

As she drives home that evening, Signithia ponders the options discussed at the meeting. "Perhaps we should increase the number of students who go to the resource room," she thinks. "But then, what does that say about our school and about what we think of our students?"

As she opens the editorial page of the local paper the next morning, Signithia is surprised to see that an editorial columnist was at last night's community meeting. She reads, curious about the columnist's perspective on the evening's debates.

Central Valley High School Faces Controversies
    Last night I attended a community meeting at Central Valley High School, at which the debates focused on what to do about the sad state of affairs at

that school. Central has been on the state watch list for at least ten years. Each successive administration struggles for a few short years to make a difference and then gives up. State achievement test results for Central's students are miserably low; lower than almost all other high schools in the region. Families who can move out of district do so, in hopes of finding more opportunities elsewhere. The audience at last night's meeting was vocal in its concerns and offered numerous suggestions for improvement. One idea, offered near the end of the meeting, struck me as interesting and a bit surprising. It was suggested that the school should increase the number of special education teachers so that more students could receive special education support, thereby increasing individualized attention. From where I sit, individualized attention sounds like a good idea. What about you, the reader? I invite your responses during the following days. Next week, I'll report those responses and offer you some final ideas on the subject.

Putting down the paper, Signithia takes her last sip of coffee and starts to get ready for the day. She is sure that there will be lively debates in the teachers' lounge and she wonders whether the recent events at school and the editorial will have any lasting effect on the quality of education at CVHS.

READER REACTIONS TO "RACE, PLACE, AND THE SEARCH FOR SOLUTIONS"

REACTIONS TO "RACE, PLACE, AND THE SEARCH FOR SOLUTIONS"

Reactions to Case 3 reveal a wide range of issues at play. Without updated textbooks and extra-curricular activities, how can the students from Central Valley compete with students from schools that have these resources in abundance? When it comes to employment or college admission, Central Valley students seem to be at a great disadvantage that has been created through their educational environment.

Complicating this picture, many of Central Valley's students are poor, too few graduate, and too many are receiving special education services, suggesting a relationship between race, class, and disability. Given the high percentage of Central students receiving special education, we must wonder whether the resources of special education are being used appropriately. After all, special education is intended for students who have significant impairments, not for students whose difficulties are the result of educational and social inequity.

When the principal calls meetings of teachers and parents, the two groups find they have similar concerns and, indeed, these same concerns are shared by teachers and parents in similar schools around the country. One questionable solution is discussed—to use special education as a means for providing the academic services students need. Parents and teachers often view special education as one answer to the kind of problems facing Central. When a community feels that it has no other choice, it is understandable that it is willing to try drastic solutions. But what might be the consequences of using special education services this way? Instead of asking what kind of difference disability makes, we might ask "What kind of difference does special education make?" Or more pointedly in this specific case, "What kind of difference does race make?"

Are Labeling and Segregation the Answer?

Desperate to see improvement in achievement, some CVHS parents push for an increase in resource room support for their children. From their perspective, the smaller class size and individualized attention common in special education resource rooms makes sense if the goal is to increase test scores. However, many respondents disagree, noting that there are other options that could yield the same benefits while avoiding the risks of labeling and segregation.

Of course the parents are pushing for more resource rooms if that means individualized instruction. This would raise test scores and make them more competitive for jobs and higher education. In my small business, I'm always hoping to get applicants who have graduated from high school with good reading and math skills. Unfortunately, I don't always find qualified employees nearby and have to search for them in other communities. This creates problems for my business. Employees who live far from work tend to miss work more often and aren't invested in the community. A lot of people forget about the implications of a poor education for employment opportunities in adulthood. If the students didn't succeed in high school, how will they succeed in the workplace? How will they qualify for the job of their choice? I agree with the parents who are pushing for special education. Why not do what it takes? If the solution is available, take advantage of it. If the students don't achieve now they could be disabled for life.

—A Parent and Small Business Owner

Why would CVHS parents and teachers want to segregate students into special education classrooms? That would double the injustice in this situation. The students are already facing poverty and a lack of resources, both of which are affecting their educational opportunities. Removing them from the general education classroom could further water down their curriculum and make them even less likely to achieve competitive skills. There must be some other options. Why not join together as a community to address the larger issues: insufficient curriculum materials, lack of resources, poverty, etc. I used to teach in a school very much like Central. We had the same problems then that Central and so many schools have now. There were parents who begged us to find their kids eligible for special education because they thought it was the only way they could get them some extra help. It often was my job to be the one to tell them their child didn't qualify and that special education couldn't help. I can tell you what happens to many of the kids who don't qualify for special education but still need additional supports, they're between a rock and a hard place. They end up in my school.

—Alternative School Principal and Special Education Teacher

Deciding to increase the number of students receiving special education support isn't as easy as snapping your fingers. Special education isn't supposed to resolve the problems caused by poverty, inadequate resources, and systemic failure. These things should be addressed at a broad social level. Students have to be found eligible for special education to get resource room support services. To be eligible, students would have to undergo testing and, if eligible, be labeled. This process is time consuming, expensive, and potentially stigmatizing. Furthermore, research shows that once a student is enrolled in special education, he rarely leaves. It's a "life sentence." Is this really what these parents want for their children? Why not push for solutions that do not require testing and labeling but that are likely to have longer term effects and could impact the entire community? Political solutions seem appropriate in this case. The community needs to pull together, insist on sufficient resources, including current textbooks, technology, and support services. If this school is unusual for the district, the district needs to funnel resources and expertise to that school. If it's a typical school for the district, then the district has some large-scale work to do, including working with the state for political solutions.

—A Teacher Educator

Of course the parents want resource room help for their children. To them, it must seem like the most obvious and fastest way to get results. The classes at CVHS are like those in the vast majority of urban schools. Parents believe that the way to get students the support they need is through smaller classes with more individualized attention. If resource rooms and special education are one way to do this, then of course parents will push for that. But parents don't always see the bigger picture, which in this case is the societal result of so many African American students in special education. I realize parents' and teachers' needs for quick solutions but in this and so many other cases, longer term solutions must be found and must get at the heart of the problem—improving the overall achievement of students in schools like CVHS and creating equity for African American students.

—An African American Community Leader

The parents pressing for special education services need to consider the long-term implications of labeling. While in the short run some students may experience a bump in achievement as a result of individualized attention, this "solution" ignores the structural issues that have created inequity at CVHS: poverty, lack of resources, over emphasis on standardized testing, children who may feel no hope for the future. Special education will be a band-aid for most of the students shunted into it as a result of these meetings. The real problems—lack of equal opportunity and lack of equal outcomes—are not solved by increasing the special education caseloads. In fact, the "solution" being touted could sabotage the school because it might look like things are better when in reality, very little has changed. Furthermore, it is likely that segregation in special education will water down the curriculum for students rather than increase their achievement and ability to do well on standardized tests. Unfortunately, the solutions likely to create real change are more complex, will take longer to succeed, and require the cooperation of people and groups at a variety of agencies, including the state.

—A State Policy Maker

What About the Students?

Where are the students' voices in the discussions at CVHS? Many of them are nearing adulthood and might feel like they have a stake in what happens in their school. One respondent noticed the absence of the students' perspectives in this case.

What strikes me as the most interesting fact in this vignette is that the students themselves were not invited to a meeting. I find that adults often either assume students are not interested in getting involved or that they will not be able to provide viable suggestions. I wonder what would have happened if students were invited to the meetings. If invited, perhaps they would feel a sense of pride in a community that they helped to recreate. Some of the most reasonable and attainable solutions would probably come from students. I find that when I involve students in the big decisions about their school, they often step up to the plate and have good ideas. When I implement ideas that students have had, students tend to be invested in the results. This is my suggestion for the CVHS community.

—A High School Principal and Parent

Most students want to learn. They want to eventually have a job and money to spend. As a student at CVHS I wonder why we have so few resources. Why can't we have fund raisers for equipment? Why can't we get sponsors? What happened to the after school activities? Does the state know it is asking for more while giving us less? Has anyone written to them about that? Spoke to a state representative? Unless something gets done quick, we will have another year of graduates who can't compete against their counterparts from other schools. I'll tell you how it feels. All that stuff about *No Child Left Behind* in the newspapers and on the television? It feels as if we have been deliberately left behind. As usual. You don't see the White schools in the other neighborhoods going without computers, books, and after school programs. They get everything. They're definitely prepared for the state exams. What can be done to make this playing field more fair?

—Michelle, a 12th Grade Student in General Education

Over-representation in Special Education

Research has shown that African American and Hispanic students are over-represented in special education. Furthermore, African American and Hispanic students receiving special education services are more likely to receive those services in segregated programs than are White or Asian students (Losen & Orfield, 2002). These historical realities suggest a strong relationship between racism and ableism in schools. Some respondents thought that this needed to be made clear to the parents who were pressing for special education services. Others contextualize the issue more broadly. One rejects the idea that racial discrimination has anything to do with this.

> I teach in a suburb just outside the city. I have found that whenever a student transfers to my school from a city school, a teacher will come to me and tell me the student should be referred to special education. As the special educator responsible for coordinating this process in my building, I am the first person general educators refer to when they think a student might be eligible. I always suggest that the teacher wait a couple of months to see if the student adjusts—but teachers are usually concerned about getting help right away. In my ten years here, this has happened almost every time the transfer student is African American. It's hard to consider my colleagues as racists but I can't think of another explanation for this. I wish I *could* think of another explanation, but I have come to know that well-intended "good people" can be racist without being aware of it. My district recently went to a policy requiring that we try interventions before we can do a referral. This means that even if teachers want to refer, they must first try to prevent a referral by changing the child's classroom environment, including their teaching methodologies. I'm anxious to see how the policy works. I hope this means that all students who are struggling or below grade level will be given a fighting chance and teachers won't use the intervention plans as a way to document student failure. I've seen that done. It happens all too often. Interventions are supposed to create a level playing field, or as level a field as possible, so that instruction is adjusted for students who have atypical learning needs. I'm keeping my fingers crossed.
>
> —A Special Education Teacher

After reading this case, I went to the special education teachers in my school and asked them what percentage of their caseload is Black. They told me 82%. That shocked me since only 63% of our school population is Black. As a Black man, I find this unacceptable. I have started addressing the issue of over-representation with my teachers. Most of them were surprised to learn about the facts of our building. When I first asked them if they thought our building followed the pattern in the rest of the country, they said no. Unfortunately, they're wrong. When I showed them the figures, the teachers were both surprised and worried about finger pointing. I could sense their discomfort. They thought I might try to blame them or find fault in what they're doing. I tried to alleviate their concerns by explaining that this phenomenon isn't limited to our school, but I'm not sure how successful I was with that. Since the meeting with the teachers, I have attended all of our school's initial IEP meetings and have made it clear to the staff that I feel personally responsible for making sure we only identify students with real impairments. From my attendance at IEPs I've learned that it's not as easy as saying "this student is Black, so we shouldn't send him to special ed." Things are more complex than that. There are some Black students who have very serious conditions and need the support of the special ed. teachers. For example, I recently attended an IEP meeting for a Black student who has a very severe learning disability. He is in 11th grade and is reading at a 1st grade level. I firmly believe that regardless of the quality of his education, he would have this condition and need special education support. At the same time, I see when other Black students do not. There's little or no difference between them and most students in general education programs. So, I am grappling with the question of how to determine when Black students are disabled by racism versus when they are actually disabled according to law.

—A High School Principal in a Large City School in the Midwest

As educators we have to ask ourselves why so many African American and Hispanic students are in special education and why so many of them are in segregated programs. We also have to ask why African American and Hispanic boys are most likely to be labeled as having emotional/behavior disorders or mental retardation. Can we honestly say that the statistics represent the innate characteristics of such students? I don't think so. And if that is not the case, then why do we have over-representation? If we are honest with ourselves as a society, we have to confront the reality that education is organized in ways that disables some students and privileges or enables others. We might even go so far as to say that it all starts with society and then trickles down to schools. Any way I look at it, I have to believe that there is something wrong with a system in which the very groups that are the most discriminated against and the least wealthy are the ones who are most likely to be segregated by special education. As a special education administrator, this knowledge makes my job very difficult because the system propels African American students toward special education and I'm always pushing back. It gets me into trouble sometimes but I can't sleep at night if I think I haven't pushed back. My district is primarily White, so I feel like I'm one of the few people in the district who can watch out for this kind of thing.

—An African American Parent and Special Education Administrator

I can't buy the explanation that some kind of discrimination is the reason for the high percentage of African American males in special education. I think there are some good explanations for why Black students might have a higher incidence of disability than White students. Perhaps the most important factor is the horrible state of urban schools. If students are raised in poverty, attend a school with a high percentage of drop-outs, and live in a neighborhood where everyone is on welfare, what can we expect? That kind of atmosphere can't be conducive to healthy development and probably causes a lot of anger. That could lead to emotional disturbances. In this case maybe the environment is *causing* the problem, but that's not discrimination. Poverty can also lead to poor health and poor medical care—and it's logical that these often lead to disability. So again, I don't see how this is a social issue. I'm all for equality but special education could be an equalizer, couldn't it? It's supposed to be. If it works, it can bring a student up to grade level.

—A General Education Teacher

OK, I buy the argument that over-representation is a problem in schools but what about under-representation? In my school, we have a large number of students from Asia, mostly India, Vietnam, Cambodia. I think they're about 18% of the student population. After reading this case study, I checked to see how many of our special education students are Asian and only 3% are Asian. Is this typical? I've always heard that Asians are the "model minority" but does that imply that they have a lower incidence of disability? Wouldn't about the same percentage of Asians be disabled as any other racial group? 37% of our student population is African American and 40% of the special education students are African American. I actually counted. That's not too off base percentage wise. This makes me question why so few of our Asian students are receiving special education. Do our teachers buy into the model minority stereotype? If not, what other explanation could there be? Is it possible that Asians are, in fact, smarter than others? I have a hard time believing that. I asked my principal about this and he said that he gets fewer discipline referrals about Asian kids, too. That surprised me and made me wonder if these things are connected in some way but I can't figure out how. Is it that the kids are different or that our attitudes about them are different?

—A High School Teacher

I am the only Latina in the Gifted Program at Evergreen High School, a school about ten minutes drive from CVHS. Since the early grades I have been in the gifted or top-track programs. My younger sister goes to CVHS, so I get to hear what it's like there. Where I am couldn't be more different. I share my books and work with her, so she is exposed to the books and work done in other places. I like it where I am but sometimes feel like the odd one out. There's only one other Latino, and he's shy. There's a few Asian-Americans, and one Black girl, but most of the students are White. Race is never really mentioned much, but I get the feeling that some students think I'm a charity case because I am on a scholarship. My best friend is White, and she's on a scholarship too. I guess I never want to discriminate, but it seems to me like most of the students in my school take it for granted. They've always expected to go to college. We don't have special ed. like in other schools, but there are a few students who have a resource room teacher once a day for support. I heard some teachers talking in the hallway once saying that there was no need for special ed. here. That left me wondering, where are the students with disabilities in my school?

—Louisa, 11th Grade General Education Student

Refocusing the Issues

Broad social issues—e.g. poverty, underfunded urban schools—influence places like Central Valley High and its problems cannot necessarily be solved by increasing the special education rosters. Funneling students into special education might help a few individuals, but those funds are limited, too. In addition, special education has its own drawbacks, including stigmatization and the need for increased revenues that could be used to attack the problem on a broader scale.

Test scores are important, but the students' mental and physical well-being has a lot to do with academic success. When the school and parents begin to build a bridge together rather than being on opposite ends, the bridge is one of success. We are not just teaching students to raise their test scores. We are preparing them for a life. After all, you can pass a test without necessarily knowing how to use the information in it! How can we better prepare kids for the ever-changing world they're entering into? What happens to the kids who got sent to special education? Will they be prepared for adult life? Will they be able to get jobs? I read recently that 85% of disabled people are unemployed or underemployed. Is this because employers won't hire the disabled or because job applicants who were in special education are unprepared for work? I'm impressed with the similarities between the two groups. Parents and teachers both identified

similar issues. The next step is for the principal to bring in community leaders, set up a planning committee that includes all the stakeholders, and
empower them to strategize about reform. We've been doing this in my city
for a few years. It's hard work that requires a lot of time and energy. We
sometimes are stumped by district policies that don't seem to make sense
for students but this is the reality of the work I do. It's one reason I decided
to go into teaching. I want to bring my expertise in community organizing
to my work as an educator.

—A Prospective High School Teacher and Community Organizer

On a personal note, this case study reminded me of a high school in the
city about 15 years ago. I knew a parent who had a son involved in the
band at a school in a wealthy district in the suburbs. The two schools—
the city and suburban schools—were having cross high school band
projects. The parent I knew was one of the committee heads. You probably
couldn't pick two schools with less in common, so it was a learning experience for all concerned. This parent told me about her first visit to the
Chicago school. The principal was giving the suburban parents a tour
of the school, when they all noticed some girls giggling by the bathroom.
When the principal asked what was going on, the girls giggled that the
pig was in the bathroom. The parent assumed she was talking about a
boy called "the pig," when a small pig on a leash came out of the bathroom.
The girls and the principal laughed and the girls picked up the pig's leash
and walked off with him. The principal explained to the confused parents
that the pig was part of their animal project. When he first came to the
school, he noticed that there were no birds. There were birds in other parts
of the neighborhood, but in the area around the school, he could only
find a few dead ones on the ground. He realized, with sadness, that some of
the students were killing them. He decided that, while academics were
important, he first had to change the school environment. His goal was to
make it a place that was physically and emotionally safe for his students. He
created quiet reading areas, he gave the students the responsibility of
planting and tending gardens, and he brought in a few animals. In being
given the responsibility of caring for the animals, students came to respect
them and take pride in their school and their own abilities. The school still
had plenty of problems, but within two years, grades went up, truancy went
down, and birds were no longer targeted. The potential CVHS solution of
placing more students in special education is only a band-aid that will create
new problems. Working with parents, teachers, and the broader community
to identify and creatively address the sources of these problems would go
much farther than putting a lot of students in special education who don't
really need to be there.

—A Pre-Service Elementary Teacher

When the Community Gets Involved

A local reporter attended one of the meetings at CVHS. He then wrote about it, thereby raising community awareness but also potentially creating tensions or controversies within the community that could interfere with the school's ability to find solutions. As in Case 2, the question of who gets to decide which solutions should be implemented emerges. In schools, who *should* get to participate in making decisions and achieving solutions? Is special education a service that a community can choose, reject, adjust to meet local needs, or is it a support based on rules and regulations about eligibility?

I was surprised to see that a local reporter had attended school meetings and was chiming in on the situation. Don't teachers have enough challenges without the press getting involved? Now the situation is broadcasted to the whole community. The school is already struggling and media interference will make it worse because everyone now has something to say about it. When I'm having problems in my classroom, I don't want others to know about it and when my school is having problems, I believe we should keep it in the family, so to speak. What's the point of parading dirty laundry in front of everyone? What good does media attention offer? This reporter did the school a disservice and the principal is implicated, as well, for allowing the reporter at the meeting in the first place. It reminds me of how school "report cards" are printed in the newspaper so that people can see which overall test results are for each school. When they started that in my state, parents spent every summer trying to get their kids into different schools based on the school report cards. My school was one of the schools that did poorly and each fall we came to school unsure of how many students would attend for the year. I know this may seem far afield from the case, which I suspect is about special education. But I think the case is about how schools decide to solve problems and who should get involved.

—A High School General Education Teacher

The federal government and the states have strict rules about how special education dollars should be spent. Special education isn't a resource that communities can tap into any way they see fit. There are eligibility requirements, procedures for determining eligibility, and other legal issues at stake. The state monitors special education and if a school did what is being suggested in this case, a monitor could discover it and there might be consequences. Funding for special education comes from the feds, the state, and the district. Whether or not students qualify for special education is based on funding and if the student meets eligibility requirements. It may seem like teachers or parents get to decide if a student receives special education services but in reality, the decision is made by policy that is much bigger than any one district or school.

—A Special Education Administrator

READER REACTIONS

SUMMARY AND ADDITIONAL QUESTIONS

Earlier we asked what kind of difference race makes and in this case it appears to make a lot of difference. Central Valley High is a failing school with desperate parents and demoralized teachers grasping at potential solutions. Their attempts are understandable because they want the best for their children and, from their perspectives, special education seems like a potential solution. They view special education's individualized attention as a means toward academic progress. This is a common belief about special education but one respondent rightly points out that "once in special education, always in special education," indicating that it might not be a solution for the problems facing Central. Stigmatized labels tend to follow a student from grade to grade, school to school. They stick fast and are hard if not impossible to remove. Furthermore, as seen in Case 2, overt ableism may be largely hidden, but is ever-present. Teachers make decisions about students based on evidence they consider valid but often it is faulty and/or the result of stereotypes. If Central students are identified for special education but do not have the conditions for which special education is intended, they will be unnecessarily labeled, might not experience the desired results, and are definitely prone to stigmatization.

Earlier we also asked what kind of difference special education makes. This case illustrates one possible *negative* difference it can make. Special education can be a solution to address significant academic difficulties for students with impairments. On the other hand, African American and Hispanic youth are significantly over-represented in special education and are therefore more likely to be in segregated programs than are White youth. In the case of race, then, special education can be a segregating institution.

Some respondents point out the social context within which this case can be understood. Central High is under-resourced and underfunded, as are many large urban schools serving low-income students. With so little money to fund general education support systems and with the complexity of the situation facing urban schools, special education supports can appear appealing. However, long-term, large-scale solutions to problems facing schools like Central need to address educational equity at a societal level. Here are some questions to consider as you reflect on this case.

1   Respondents vary in whether or not they agree that race and disability are connected in cases like this. What do you think? Does race make a difference when it comes to disability? If so, how?

2   It is established that racial over-representation has existed in special education as long as special education has existed. What are the consequences of this? Does special education give students who struggle a chance at success or hold them back? Is it a support service that can make a difference in either direction, i.e. to enable or further disable a student in their educational experience?

3   Some respondents suggest that racism is a factor in over-representation. What do you think? If it *is* a factor, how can a teacher combat racism so that s/he does not contribute to over-representation? What could be done at the school level? The district level? The state level?

4   This case raises the question of the purpose of special education and who gets to decide whether special education is an appropriate service. What do you believe to be the purpose of special education? Who do you think should determine special education eligibility?

5   In combating over-representation, some educators—such as a principal featured earlier—fear a loss of special education services for African American and Latino students. Does addressing such a policy risk "throwing the baby out with the bathwater"? Can a balance of equally represented students according to race be reached within special education? Given discrepancies among wealth and educational supports provided within/to families, can schools be held as the primary institutions to close "the achievement gap"?

6   To what degree are Gifted and Talented programs exclusive? Why are Asians and Euro-Americans over-represented while African Americans, Latinos, and Native Americans are under-represented? In your opinion, does the broad concept of inclusion described in Case 1 incorporate children identified as gifted and talented? If so, why? If not, why not?

7   One respondent noted what may appear to many as a paradox: "Good people can be racist." What do you think she meant? What are some examples in which individuals can be subconsciously or subtly racist, without realizing or recognizing the source of their ideas?

8   What are some of the relationships touched upon in this case study that show interconnections between personal, institutional, societal, and historical racism?

INTRODUCTION TO CASE 4

Teachers begin their careers with expectations formed as a result of their formal preparation in a teacher education program. In addition, their own school experiences *as a student* also contribute to their ideas about teaching. However, teacher education can never fully prepare someone for the realities of the classroom, and ideas about teaching gleaned as a student can be unrealistic. This is particularly true in the case of disability, a form of diversity that exists in most public school classrooms and many private school classrooms. In Case 4, middle school teacher, Martin Louis, is learning these lessons first hand. As a new teacher, he is finding that some things are not what he expected. As Martin struggles with the typical novice challenges—lesson planning, classroom discipline, school politics—he also faces the realization that his students are not what he expected them to be. As a student himself, Martin remembers being studious, curious, and intellectually invested. This was particularly true in his social studies classes with his favorite teacher. He remembers that teacher as a gifted instructor who fully engaged students in almost every class. But in his first year of teaching, Martin is faced with students who do not do their homework, cannot read the textbook, and require him to prioritize a significant amount of time to be spent upon discipline. Martin feels resentful that these students are taking so much time away from what he considers the real job of teaching. The lessons Martin must learn are those facing all new teachers. He finds himself confronting his assumptions about his students, his role as a teacher, his understanding of responsibilities in planning to teach, and his own ethics of teaching.

CASE 4: "MARTIN LOUIS, *SPECIAL* EDUCATOR?"

Martin Louis has dreamed of being a social studies teacher ever since high school, when he had Mr. Johnson for U.S. Government. Mr. Johnson was one of those teachers who could make almost any subject interesting and for Martin, U.S. Government came alive that year. Now, in his first year of teaching social studies at a large metropolitan middle school, Martin is facing the same challenges confronting all new teachers such as classroom management, assessment, pressure from federal and state mandates, grading, school politics, and so on. At first, Martin thought that things would settle down at some point during the year and he would be able to teach like he remembers Mr. Johnson teaching. Mr. Johnson's classes always seemed trouble-free. Students rarely disrupted class. Everyone turned in their homework. Entire class periods were spent with students and teacher fully engaged in learning.

Martin is disappointed to find that by mid-year, he's still spending a lot of time with classroom management. His mentor teacher, Mrs. Booker, gives him advice and he incorporates her ideas into his teaching but it seems as though much of each class is spent trying to control students, keeping them in their seats, and monitoring them to be sure they do their assignments. Martin's detailed lesson plans developed from thematic units he designs and aligns with state learning standards appear wasted because so much time is spent on what feels like babysitting. In a mentoring conference with Mrs. Booker, Martin admits that he has experienced some progress in recent weeks. The classroom management system Mrs. Booker suggested seems to be giving him more time to teach. Students are turning in homework with greater frequency, although there's still room for more improvement. Martin also says that student grades during this marking period will be better this time. To Martin and Mrs. Booker, this suggests that his teaching is improving. However, one thing still bothers Martin and he finally admits it in the mentoring conference.

"I entered the profession to teach general education, not special education," he says. "First and foremost, I consider myself a social studies teacher and I want to focus my teaching efforts on content and preparing students for the demands of the state tests and, eventually, high school."

"Teaching isn't just about being a subject matter specialist, Martin," suggests Mrs. Booker. "It's also important to know and value our students as individuals in order to adjust our teaching to meet their individual needs."

"I guess I realize that. But I imagined that my classes would have one or two special education students. I never thought that up to a third of a class would be in special education," he sighs.

"They're not 'in special education,' Martin," Mrs. Booker responds. "They're in your class."

Martin then points out the fact that his fifth period class of 7th graders is co-taught with a special education teacher and almost half of the students are receiving special education support. He is convinced that most of his difficulties as a new teacher can be attributed to the fact that so many children in his classes are special education students—and he is not trained as a special educator.

"I resent having to water down my curriculum because the special education students can't keep up with the regular curriculum," complains Martin.

Mrs. Booker asks, "Give me an example of what you do to water down the curriculum."

Martin describes a recent current events lesson he prepared that relied on a series of short articles from local newspapers, a PBS special on the same event, and students writing letters to the editor of the school paper.

"Students were to read the articles the night before this class session," he points out. "But many of the special education students could not read the newspaper article, even though it was the best text to use for this lesson. So they came unprepared to class. I had to spend most of the period teaching them the content of the article that they were supposed to read the night before."

"Couldn't you have found a text that they *were* able to read? Perhaps something in *USA Today* or the *Weekly Reader*, which are both written at a lower reading level than our newspaper? Perhaps there was something online that would have worked. Did you do a search to see if you could find something?" asks Mrs. Booker. "Or, you could have collaborated with your co-teacher, who might have some ideas."

"That wasn't the only problem," answered Martin. "The social studies concepts in the lesson were related to concepts in previous lessons and few of the special education students remembered those concepts. I had to re-teach the concepts, too."

Martin then describes the lesson as "dragging on without the energy and conceptual depth that I had intended because we had to move so slowly for the special education students."

"I can see that we have a lot of work to do, Martin," sighs Mrs. Booker. "Let's get Sheree involved."

At the next mentoring conference, Mrs. Booker and Martin invite the special education teacher, who co-teaches with Martin, to join them. Sheree Tyler has been teaching special education for five years. She is an energetic, upbeat woman who seems to have a wealth of information about how to organize a lesson to accommodate all students.

Martin shares his concerns with both colleagues, particularly his concerns about the curriculum and the pressures he feels as the time nears for the state achievement tests.

"In the end, I guess I'm also concerned about whether my classes will be singled out as not making enough progress," he admits, "and whether this will affect my ability to keep my job as an untenured teacher."

Sheree jumps in, asking, "When it comes to planning lessons for your students, what is your greatest concern?"

"Well, I think it's that I'm not sure what each student can and cannot do and even if I knew that, I wouldn't know how to plan a lesson to accommodate everyone."

"Are you willing to learn?" asks Mrs. Booker.

"Is my experience this year pretty typical for a middle school teacher?" asks Martin.

"Yes," chimed in both Sheree and Mrs. Booker.

"If my lessons are based on what all middle school students should know about social studies, then how can I rationalize changing what I'm doing? Don't I have to hold everyone to the same requirements?" asks Martin.

"It depends on what you mean by requirements," answers Mrs. Booker. "If you mean that everyone must do the same thing at the same time in the same way, then the answer is no. As a teacher, you can adjust and accommodate based on individual student needs. Naturally, you have to design your lessons around our curriculum standards, but it is appropriate to vary teaching strategies, curriculum materials, and student activities to make sure all students are being successful."

"We want all teachers to have high expectations for our students," says Sheree, "but we also want teachers to create opportunities for success for every student in the classroom. By planning lessons and choosing curriculum materials—bearing students with diverse abilities in mind—you can create success while also having high expectations."

"I still don't get it," responds Martin. "It seems to me that our state's curriculum standards are clear that specific requirements must be met and that we are accountable for making sure students meet those requirements."

"Yes," Mrs. Booker conceded. "But teaching as a profession holds us accountable for certain things, too."

"Like being student-centered," adds Sheree.

"And creating a sense of community and collaboration in our classrooms so that our students grow to become good citizens," says Mrs. Booker.

"And—" Sheree doesn't get to finish.

"I'm sorry," Martin cuts her off, "but I think the teaching profession holds subject matter teachers accountable for imparting content knowledge to students. A college degree is required for almost any job above minimum wage. If students can't handle the subject matter, then I think that's why we have special education." Martin is firm on this point. At this point the bell rings and each teacher returns to his or her classroom.

A few weeks later, Mrs. Booker brings the state's curriculum standards for middle school social studies to their next meeting. She asks Martin to select a goal he is currently working on with his classes. Martin chooses "Understand political systems, with an emphasis on the United States." He then indicates that the standard he is teaching this week is "understanding election processes and responsibilities of citizens."

"This is a relevant standard since the elections are only a few weeks away," says Mrs. Booker. "How are you approaching this with your students?"

"Every day I bring in one or two newspaper clippings that are appropriate to the standard. Since we're in the middle of a heated campaign for mayor, the issues are in the news a lot. I require that students bring in one newspaper clipping a week that addresses the campaign issues. They share their clippings in small groups. This week, we're concentrating on how students view the issues and who they would vote for if they could vote."

"That sounds exciting and timely, Martin. You've described activities that all students can participate in. Regardless of what a student brings in, it will be relevant to the standard if it is about the election process. Every student in your class will be able to take a position, whether or not they understand the issues in depth. I'm interested in how the students are responding," says Mrs. Booker.

Martin is happy to talk about his latest successes. "Most of them are doing OK. Sheree has helped me think of ways to be flexible and use various strategies to try to reach all the students. The most useful thing I'm doing is allowing choices whenever possible; choices in assignments, choices in materials. At first, I considered focusing on the national elections but Sheree convinced me that the students would be more interested in and better informed about local politics."

"Good idea. Generally speaking, middle school students do seem more interested in local issues although there are also national issues they find compelling. They see these things being discussed on TV. Keeping this in mind can help you focus your lessons in the right direction." Mrs. Booker seems to approve. "Let's try another one."

This time Martin chooses the goal, "Understand social systems with an emphasis on the United States." "We'll be working on this goal next month after the elections," he says.

"Which standard will you start with?" asks Mrs. Booker.

"I'm thinking of starting with 'understand how social systems form and develop over time' because I think my students will be interested in a benchmark under that standard." Martin points to the benchmark and reads, "'explain how diverse groups have contributed to US social systems over time.' This means that students need to know how groups of people interact and relate to one another in our society. I have a student who just moved here from India. There are a growing number of Indian immigrants in our school and I thought it would be interesting to focus on the contributions of South Asians to our city and state."

"Great idea!" Mrs. Booker exclaims. "Now let's think about curriculum resources that would represent a wide range of literacy levels to accommodate the diverse abilities in your room."

Martin lists his ideas. "Newspapers; movies like *Bend it Like Beckham* and *Slumdog Millionaire*; the Internet; Mrs. Vyas, our school librarian is from Mumbai; our textbook; magazine articles."

"Yes," Mrs. Booker agrees. "You see that the standards and benchmarks do not require specific curriculum materials. They only specify content knowledge. The textbook works for students who are able to read fairly well. But you need other resources to add interest and increase motivation for all students, and to provide accessible information to those students who cannot read well, like Mario, your student with Down Syndrome. How will you assess student achievement of this benchmark? Again, remember that the goals, standards, and benchmarks don't specify what types of assessments you must use."

"Wow, I hadn't thought about how much wiggle room I have. I could ask students to talk about what they learned. I could have them be a movie critic. I could have them do an archive search for newspaper articles about South Asian contributions and then write a historical essay. I could certainly have them do Internet searches. This could free me from having to prepare and grade a multiple choice or essay test after the unit."

"All very good ideas, Martin." Mrs. Booker seems encouraged by Martin's ideas.

"I feel more comfortable with my options," Martin says. "But I wish someone had told me that being a teacher required more than mastery of my subject. And I'm not sure how well this style of teaching will prepare students for the standardized tests that are coming up, nor am I sure how I should be grading students, since everyone could be doing very different things."

"Let's take things one step at a time, Martin."

READER REACTIONS TO "MARTIN LOUIS, *SPECIAL* EDUCATOR?"

REACTIONS TO "MARTIN LOUIS, *SPECIAL* EDUCATOR?"

Through his collaboration with Mrs. Booker and Sheree, Martin is learning that teaching is much more complex than he had originally thought and his responsibilities are broader than initially anticipated. He may likely be wondering if knowledge of his subject is sufficient for achieving the kind of success as a teacher that he had hoped to achieve. Martin struggles with this dilemma because his passion for social studies is one of the main reasons he went into teaching. He is fortunate to have two experienced teachers to lean on in his first year. While Martin has a good grasp of social studies, Sheree has knowledge of students with special educational needs, and Mrs. Booker is a mature teacher who is experienced in designing a curriculum for all students.

This case illustrates many of the curriculum and instruction challenges facing all teachers in diverse schools. For example, Martin seems to be struggling with a basic premise of modifying curriculum or instruction to accommodate all students. He wonders when and how to do this. At the same time he does see a connection between a teacher's flexibility and increased student engagement. Still, he's left asking: Where does a teacher draw the line and say, "This is too much. It's beyond the scope of my responsibility or ability." Here, we ask the same question, but rephrased: To what extent is the subject matter teacher responsible for students who are still developing basic skills?

Whose Responsibility?

A basic question Martin appears to struggle with is whether or not it is his responsibility to adjust his expectations and pedagogy based on the skill level of special education students. His training as a social studies teacher has emphasized the importance of subject matter but it also probably introduced him to child and adolescent development, an important knowledge set for a middle school teacher. That said, his college training may not have prepared him for the diversity of student abilities he faces now.

This case illustrates my most basic worries as a future teacher. I have kids in a public school and I'm a parent volunteer there so I know that classrooms today are extremely diverse. I can't imagine how I'm going to juggle everything. I watch my children's teachers and think they do a marvelous job, but I don't know all the details of how they manage. I don't see what goes on behind the scenes, how much time they spend planning and the difficulties they may be having. Martin didn't study special education; he studied how to be a social studies teacher. He knows the middle school social studies curriculum and the state standards. Martin doesn't seem convinced that subject matter should be modified by the accommodations needed by some students. He questions the extent to which he should be adjusting his expectations. On the other hand, Mrs. Booker, an experienced teacher, is pushing him to make these adjustments. So I'm torn. It seems that she wouldn't be assigned to mentor him if she wasn't on the right track with this. Honestly, I'm not sure where I stand on this issue.

—A Prospective Teacher

Martin seems to be persuaded by Mrs. Booker near the end of the case and is adjusting his instructional strategies and choices. He begins to use texts that are written at a lower reading level but that still have content consistent with his curriculum goals. He feels like there's "wiggle room" that he didn't think he had. But he's still wondering about the degree of his responsibility to meet the needs of special education students whose skills are below grade level. He knows that Sheree has been trained as a special education teacher and I think he *still* believes that special education students are primarily her responsibility because she knows how to create a curriculum that meets their needs. After all, Martin doesn't necessarily have the skills that Sheree has. As the parent of a special education student, I want my child to have the best trained teachers she can get. I want her teachers to understand her disability and to be able to use teaching strategies that are appropriate for her.

—A Parent

I'm surprised to see that Martin has entered teaching thinking he's not responsible for the learning of students with disabilities in his classroom. Students with disabilities have as much right to be in his classroom as any other students. And general education teachers like Martin should wake up to the fact that students with disabilities are not going to disappear. They are in almost every class whether the teacher knows it or not. Pretending they don't exist or that teachers aren't responsible for their learning isn't going to make them go away. On the contrary, it might make them fail because certain classrooms can be difficult or uncomfortable places for them to be. Not working with students who have IEPs might result in some of them being transferred into segregated programs. But some will remain and continue to challenge teachers to accept responsibility for them. Martin's teacher education program should have prepared him for this. Doesn't every education student have to take at least one class about students with disabilities?

—A Special Education Teacher

Martin's district has provided him with a mentor, Mrs. Booker, to help him adjust to his new job. And, fortunately, he has Sheree as a co-teacher, who has expertise to balance his. I hope he takes advantage of the opportunities they are giving him. The district has done a good job supporting Martin as a novice teacher. For whatever reason, many districts don't provide these supports and teachers like Martin struggle without backup. All too often in those cases the students with disabilities are blamed instead of the lack of support systems.

—A General Education Teacher

While I agree that Martin has responsibility for all students in his classroom, I believe that Sheree and Mrs. Booker are also responsible because all adults in the school are responsible for all students. They say "It takes a village," and I believe that. Teaching is too complex and schools are too diverse to hold one person responsible for the learning of a classroom. I'm guessing that in Martin's classrooms, there are students who need bilingual or ESL teachers, school social workers, parents, and even other students. A school is a community and everyone bears some responsibility for what happens in it.

—A School Counselor

Curriculum of In/Exclusion

As a subject matter specialist, the curriculum is one of Martin's primary emphases and areas of expertise. Respondents have a lot to say about the curriculum, whether or not it is possible to meet the needs of all students in a classroom like Martin's, how to create a curriculum of inclusion, and the problems of exclusion.

Martin's initial approach to curriculum is to *unintentionally* exclude some students while including others. The students who were excluded are those whose skills aren't up to what Martin considers an appropriate level. It's likely that a sizable number of these students aren't just special education students but are also students who do not have disabilities. Students struggle for many different reasons, not just because of a disability. By excluding students Martin views as disabled, he's also probably excluding other students too. This means that Martin has included *some* or perhaps *most* but not *all* students without disabilities. Martin revises his lessons over the course of this case study and I'm glad to see that. But in the end he is still questioning whether or not his subject matter, as he understands it, should be "modified" to fit the needs of students. He's wrestling with what appears to him as his original way of thinking, the opposite idea: shouldn't students be changed to meet the content? Rather than emphasizing his subject, I'd like to see him emphasize understanding of concepts and students achieving learning goals that are possible for them as individuals. I admit this is a tricky balancing act. It's easy to underestimate students when individualizing because individualization tends to focus on student deficits and doesn't generally aim high enough.

—A Researcher and Teacher Educator

The curriculum is too often used as a way to weed out unwanted students. Perhaps Martin subconsciously learned to do this in his own life as a teacher or perhaps he had models of it in his teacher education program. But using the curriculum to exclude students is ethically bankrupt. If a teacher is doing it intentionally, which I *don't* believe Martin is doing, then he is miseducating everyone. When I see situations in which the curriculum excludes some students and not others, I think of the messages this sends to all students. Of course, the excluded students learn life lessons about their place in the classroom, but their place in school tends to reflect their place in the larger society. Both included and excluded students, whether they then realize it or not, are learning lessons about who counts and who doesn't, who's worth it and who isn't, who is valued and who is not. These lessons carry over into adult life, at work, in social relationships, in leisure activities. The curriculum is a powerful means for teaching life lessons.

—A Curriculum Consultant

Mrs. Booker has some good advice for Martin. I like her ideas for how to plan lessons that are inclusive. In my classroom I always anticipate that I will have students with a wide range of abilities and I plan my lessons from the ground up to meet all students' needs. I practice Universal Design—or UD for short—which I learned in my teacher ed. program. In Universal Design, you start in the beginning to plan for all students instead of planning for some and then making modifications later. My prof called modifications after the fact "retro-fitting." UD appeals to me as a teacher and also as the mother of a child with Down Syndrome.

—An Elementary Teacher

Mrs. Booker is asking too much of Martin. It's his first year of teaching. He's struggling with many different things. But he knows his subject. Why not let him practice what he knows and give him time to adjust to his first teaching job before expecting him to learn new skills? The standards are his guide, not the students' deficits. He should maintain his high standards and most students will achieve them. Those who don't . . . well that's what special education is for.

—A High School Teacher

What is a Teacher's Role?

Martin struggles with how far he wants to go in accommodating his students. This is a similar struggle to the one facing the teachers in "Inclusion Tension." In Case 1, teachers asked about the degree to which their responsibilities would expand and perhaps become too much for them. As veteran teachers, they were also experiencing some resistance to change but even Martin, as a new teacher, is resisting change in his *idea* of teaching as well as the *tasks* of teaching.

> This case suggests one of the most difficult challenges of inclusive education—where does the teacher or the school team or the parent say, "That's more than we can do"? Is there a point at which the challenges are too great and it just isn't possible, the range of needs is too broad and we can't meet them all in one classroom? I believe that point exists but I don't know where it is. It depends on so many factors: the students, classroom dynamics, the teacher(s), the support systems or lack thereof, the district and its resources, the administration and its commitment or lack thereof, the parents and their preferences or resistance, the subject and grade level, and much more. Where should Martin draw the line? It's unclear in the information provided but it *is* clear to me that he hasn't reached the line, wherever it might be. He hasn't tapped out his support system. Mrs. Booker and Sheree still have more to give. Martin doesn't seem to have reached a personal roadblock. He still seems able to grow and change. His grade level makes it easier to be inclusive than it would be in high school, when academics become more rigorous. So I'm not sure where Martin's line would be drawn, if he would in the end draw a line.
>
> —A Teacher Educator

Students can tell the teachers who care and who don't. The ones that care will not give up on you. They will show you how to do things three times if they have to. More sometimes, until the student "gets it." They will show you different ways to do your work. It's not just all about books, books, books. They change things around so we work in groups, debate, act things out, present, draw. Those teachers still want us to work hard and pass our tests, but they do it in different ways.

—A Middle School Student

Martin seems to think he has a choice about whether to plan for *all* of his students. I believe he's mistaken about this. A teacher shouldn't be allowed to cherry pick and decide who's in and who's out, who he'll plan lessons for and who he won't. Where is the policy that teachers get to make those decisions? Isn't a teacher responsible for the learning of every student sitting in his classroom? But even as I ask these questions I'm now wondering, who *does* get to make these decisions? As a trained historian, I ask this in light of our understanding of the US as a democracy and public schools as democratic institutions. If schools *are* democratic institutions, then who *does* get to decide who is included and who isn't, who teachers teach and who they don't teach, who is segregated and who isn't? These are difficult questions that I believe we must confront as a society, not as individual teachers or single schools or districts. In a democracy, who decides?

—A Parent and Prospective High School History Teacher

Teachers can only do so much. They are human and they have limitations. If we want teachers who don't have limits, then we need to figure out how to make them experts at everything or we need to invent robots with computer brains that hold information about every type of student and every possible strategy for every possible student.

—A Teacher

This case is a good illustration of the importance of collaboration. Without Sheree and Mrs. Booker, Martin would struggle more, take a lot longer to figure things out, and probably wouldn't feel very successful at this point. Their experience and expertise makes him a better teacher and collectively, they are able to do more than any of them could alone. When teachers rely on one another's expertise, they improve their own skills and effectiveness. I think of this as capacity building. It means that teachers or schools improve their ability to serve students and society at large when they work together, making use of their joint efforts. Even if a school doesn't use co-teaching as a model, as does Martin's school, teachers can still collaborate. The key is whether or not they are open to sharing their concerns and needs with their colleagues. Being open can be difficult at first because it can make a person feel vulnerable and open to criticism. But if the collaboration is supportive, avoids unnecessary criticism, and focuses on what can be done to be effective, then the relationship is worthwhile.

—A Principal

READER REACTIONS

SUMMARY AND ADDITIONAL QUESTIONS

Martin entered teaching thinking that his passion for his subject would make him successful and he assumed that his students would share that passion, as he did at their age. His dilemma is an ethical one in that he is wondering whether it is his responsibility to plan curriculum for students receiving special education support. He has to decide whether he is respons-ible to facilitate effective learning for the *greatest number* of students— which may or may not include disabled students—or *all* students. If he chooses to teach for the greatest good, he has to decide who belongs and who doesn't belong in the greatest good category, which typically refers to the majority. He then must decide what teaching to the greatest good looks and feels like and what he might do about the students who do not belong in what he considers the "greatest good" category. What will become of them? Martin might also contemplate whether his ethical responsibility is toward the common good—what is good for *all* students, in spite of the challenges this poses. If this is his position, then Martin has to decide what the common good looks and feels like as a teacher and for his students and how he might achieve it. Finally, Martin might also be feeling an ethical responsibility to his discipline—social studies—and to passing on knowl-edge of the discipline to the next generation. If so, he has to make decisions about the boundaries, standards, content, and flexibility of the discipline. While these ethical positions are somewhat contradictory, we might also consider the ways in which they overlap and create a unique ethical context in which there are few easy answers but within which he has to make ethical judgments. For example, Martin may decide that he is interested in the common good but that he is also responsible to the state to assure that his students meet content area standards. What does that mean for the common good? Or he may decide that his ethical responsibility is primarily to his discipline. What does that mean for students who are struggling but who do not have support from special education services? Or he may decide that, in a democracy, the different needs of all students should be considered equally. How might that stance impact important curriculum decisions? These are only three of the many questions raised by this case. What follows are some more questions.

1   Respondents disagree about Martin having the authority to decide whether or not he is responsible for all students in his classroom. What is your position? What authority does a teacher have to decide these matters? If s/he has some authority, how are those parameters defined?

2   Assuming teachers do have the authority to decide who they are responsible to teach, how should they make that decision? What criteria should be used? Where is the line drawn? To what kind of students should general educators be responsible? Why do you take these positions?

3   Consider the ways in which Martin's curriculum decisions included or excluded students from full participation in the curriculum. Thinking about the subject(s) you plan to teach or are teaching, in what ways could your curriculum decisions inadvertently include or exclude? Which learners would you include and how? Which learners would you exclude and how? Use specific examples.

4   Thinking about the three ethical positions above—the greatest good, the common good, and the discipline's good—which position do you take and why? How does that position get enacted in your teaching? What does that position look like in curriculum decisions you might make? Who or what becomes invisible when teachers take that position? Who or what becomes visible when teachers take that position?

5   If you haven't yet considered the ethics of teaching in relation to society at large rather than a single classroom, consider your answers to the following questions for society at large. Who gains the most from each of the three ethical positions? In other words, who benefits when teachers teach for the greatest good? The common good? The discipline's good? Provide support for your answer.

6   One respondent spoke of Universal Design. In what ways can this idea be useful to all teachers? How might this theory look in practice? What might it look like if Martin teaches a unit on The American Civil War or The Civil Rights Movement?

READER REACTIONS TO THE FOUR CASES

REACTIONS TO THE FOUR CASES

Most respondents addressed specific cases but a few considered the intersections, relationships, connections, and disconnections between all four cases. For these respondents, the cases meshed in interesting and divergent ways. Where one respondent viewed the cases as bringing together a number of important educational issues of concern for all teachers, another thinks there is a disconnect between the elementary and secondary cases. A third respondent focused on the political issues running through all four cases.

Initially, I didn't see the connection between the cases but as I reflected further, I realized that they all pose the question of who belongs in general education? In Case 1, some teachers and perhaps some parents question whether or not disabled students should be included in general education classrooms. Their questions about the degree of support students need, how specific supports might change teacher roles and responsibilities, and whether or not they are prepared for such a task are similar to Martin's questions as an individual in Case 4. In some ways, I think that Martin and the teachers at Villa Nueva are struggling with the same issues as those in cases 2 and 3: What should a school community look like? Who should be in classrooms together and what are the consequences of the decisions that are made in this regard? How do educators make decisions about such important matters? I wonder if the decisions are usually made by tradition—"This is how we've always done it." Surely, someone must come along at some point and say "No. This isn't how we're going to do it anymore"? When I was in school, things were very different than they are now. In those days, I never saw special education students because they weren't even attending school in my building. But today, special education students are going to school with everyone else. Is that a good thing? I think so, but I'm also not one hundred percent sure. Inclusion has certainly changed the way teachers teach. It has changed the tenor of school buildings. But other things have changed drastically too. Back in the day, most of the children in my school spoke English only—or if they spoke another language, it was Spanish. Today, my school has students who speak 52 different languages! Sometimes when I think about that I'm amazed that we accomplish anything other than teaching English as a second language. So, what I'm trying to say is that I don't think these case studies present something that's entirely new. Schools have had to consider integrating other groups, such as immigrants from the time public schooling started, girls since the early twentieth century, and African American students after *Brown*. The difference here is that the learning needs of the students might be somewhat different. However, there are other things that are the same: the need to belong, to have friends, to engage with the curriculum, to grow.

—A Teacher with 35 Years of Experience

Each of these cases raises important issues but I think that there is a difference between the implications in elementary and secondary schools. The
teachers at Villa Nueva and Forest Run have more flexibility than do the
teachers at Central Valley High and at Martin's school. The tensions
resulting from pressure to make academic progress are evident in the last
two cases. Secondary teachers don't have the flexibility to make significant
adjustments to content area standards. On the contrary, elementary teachers
have less pressure and a greater ability to accommodate individual learners.
Middle school teachers are under pressure to prepare students for high
school. High school teachers are under pressure to prepare students for
college, trade school, or competitive employment. Not only are the pressures greater, but they're compounded by secondary teachers having many
more students and for shorter periods of time. Elementary teachers are able
to get to know their students more intimately. I guess my main point is that
while inclusion might be a good thing in theory, its implementation at the
secondary level is much more complicated than at the elementary level—as
the performance gap simply grows wider and wider.

                                                —A High School Teacher

I have to mention the politics behind these case studies. At first I read each
one separately and thought they weren't connected at all, but in our educational foundations course we've been learning about the politics of education. By the time I reached the fourth case study about Martin I realized that
politics is a theme running through all four cases because each case is about
who has the power to decide how things get done in schools. In each case,
the politics are both explicit and implicit. Explicitly, the people involved are
debating options of how things should be done and what might happen in
each scenario. The implicit politics are the most interesting to me.
Underlying each case are the assumptions people make about how things
should or shouldn't be done and the unconscious decisions made without
realizing why they are being made. In Case 1, teachers are surprised at the
idea that special education students are to be included in their classrooms
but they don't realize that their surprise is based on how widespread exclusion is not recognized as such. In Case 4, Martin does a similar thing. He
starts teaching making assumptions about his role and responsibilities, but
his decisions, too, are based in a politics of exclusion. As an African
American male who was in special education from grades 3 to 12, Case 3
really got me. Talk about the politics of silence! In that case, people are
actually considering actively *disabling* students, because the school needs
to make progress? Get real. I know the feeling of being silenced. I felt that
way in 3rd grade when I was put in special education. My grades were OK,
not great, but OK. My teacher thought I was a troublemaker, a behavior
problem. At least that's the message I got. Case 2 and Shelly's attitude

toward Jesse is so similar to my own experience. I often wonder, will I do the same thing? Will I make assumptions about students and draw faulty conclusions based on those? Will I harm my students? I hope not.

—A Prospective Middle School Teacher

I am struck by what I see as ableism running throughout each case. While the second case is explicitly about ableism, I also see ableism in teachers' responses to inclusion in Case 1, in the way people in Case 3 are so quick to disable minority students by using special education as a solution to social inequity, and in Case 4 the way Martin resists creating a curriculum that's accessible to all students. I like to approach cases like these by turning things upside down. What would happen if a group of teachers in a public school would complain about including students with blue eyes? What if they went to the principal and said, "I don't want *those students* in my classroom. They are too different from other students. I don't know what to do with students with blue eyes." People would be outraged. So why don't people get outraged when teachers say they can't teach disabled students?

—A Teacher Educator

II

PUBLIC ARGUMENTS

Part I of this book contains case studies that speak to some of the central issues of disability and teaching in U.S. public schools. When all responses are taken as a whole, the cases share some overarching themes, including the following.

1. Teaching and community: How do people in school (teachers, administrators, students) relate to one another and to the broader community? How does the school reflect the larger community or the community's vision of itself?

2. Teaching and cultural values: Who is given privilege, what and who are given importance, what are the purposes for education and how are they prioritized?

3. Teaching and politics: Who has authority to make decisions about 1 and 2 above and with what aims in mind; how do teachers influence or participate in the politics of education?

4. Teaching and ethics: Whose needs are served, toward what good are these needs served and within what ethical framework does the teacher make decisions?

In *Culture and Teaching*, the second book in this series, Liston and Zeichner (1996) note that "education in most democracies is a *publicly funded, state-supported endeavor*," and that "public schools are *public* institutions" (p. 55). In other words, schools are intended to serve the public good, and because they do so, we must consider the following questions: (1) who constitutes "the public"? Who is included in and excluded from this category? Why are they included or excluded?; and (2) what is meant by "the public good"? Who gets to decide what it is? How can it be achieved? These questions invoke existing tensions that are raised when "the public good" is considered. For example, are schools serving the public good when they are designed with particular kinds of students in mind, and with the specific intention of excluding or segregating others? Or, if not designed with the specific *intention* of excluding, what about the unintentional exclusion that occurs as a result of the school's design, curriculum, and/or instruction? How does a local community agree on what constitutes the public good and does the local public good serve the national public good? Furthermore, given the very real state of limited public resources, we ask: how are resources allocated? Who gets to make allocation decisions? On what criteria are those decisions made? Who does and does not benefit from the allocation decisions?

In *Gender and Teaching*, another book in this series, Maher and Ward (2002) write that "most teachers are not taught to think about the implications of what they do in their classrooms for their schools, their communities, or their country" (p. xix). The Reflective Teaching series fills this gap by urging consideration of such things. In the case of *Disability and Teaching*, you have been asked to reflect on your beliefs about disability and teaching and the ways in which those beliefs could affect your practice as a teacher, *all* of your students, and society as a whole. Teacher education often falls short in this regard because it too seldom provides opportunities for teachers to consider the ways in which they themselves serve society at large.

In Part II, we use the issues and themes raised by the case studies to articulate, compare, and contrast three public arguments that can be used to analyze these cases. We have labeled these three public arguments as follows: "A Conservative View: Rewarding Achievement, Maintaining Tradition," "A Liberal-Progressive View: Celebrating Diversity, Creating Equity," and "A Disability-Centered View: Acknowledging Difference, Deconstructing Normalcy." In the Preface we noted that these categories can be misleading and used the example of conservative President George H. W. Bush signing civil rights legislation, the Americans with Disabilities Act, into law. We also referred to the importance of understanding political events in their historical context and used the example of the *Individuals with Disabilities Education Improvement Act* (2004) (IDEA). When the IDEA was first enacted in 1975 (then the *Education for All Handicapped*

Children Act, also known as P.L. 94–142), it was considered quite progressive, perhaps even radical in the eyes of some. It was, after all, the first time that disabled school age children were *guaranteed the right* to what the law termed a "free, appropriate public education." In contrast, using the standards of many people in the radical disability-centered view, the IDEA represents a conservative stance toward disability because it allows for segregation based on what IDEA calls the "continuum of services" that includes segregated schools and institutional placements. So we use the three categories—Conservative, Liberal-Progressive, Disability-Centered—with caution, and ask that you do as well.

In the three sections that follow we provide an overview of the lens with which each public argument might examine the four cases in Part I. The conservative interest in upholding traditional values is skeptical about the extent to which the purposes and conditions of schooling should be changed based on the interests of a single social group; in this case, disabled students. Often associated with conservatism, meritocracy is the organization of society based on perceived intellectual ability or competence. A meritocracy is a competitive society in which positions of leadership, wealth, and status are assumed to be the result of merit based on talent, motivation, and effort. The liberal-progressive public argument posits that we are a society full of diverse social groups identified by race, gender, country of origin, language, religion, socio-economic status, sexual orientation, etc., and that our diversity is cause for celebration. The liberal-progressive position tends to be critical of meritocratic social systems and argues instead for equity in spite of differences in perceived competence. Disabled people can be found adhering to each of the previous two public arguments. There are many disabled conservatives, such as former Senator Bob Dole whose injury in the Vietnam War resulted in paralysis in his right hand. There also are many disabled liberal-progressives, including former Senator Max Cleland, also a Vietnam War veteran, who lost both legs to a grenade. This makes the third public argument—the disability-centered position—somewhat confusing. As with any other social group, disabled people do not agree on all political points, nor do they share the same values, goals, or sense of themselves as disabled people. Setting aside this reality, the third public argument examines important issues raised in the cases by placing disability in the center of the discussion, making disability the touchstone or critical feature of each issue. When that is done, the view is quite different than from within the other two public arguments.

After each public argument we propose additional questions and issues to reflect upon and hope that you explore them in discussions in class or with colleagues. We link the questions and issues to those raised by the four cases in Part I and encourage you to further extend the linkages more broadly than we have.

A "CONSERVATIVE VIEW": REWARDING ACHIEVEMENT, MAINTAINING TRADITION

Introduction

Our country was founded on the value of hard work by people who rejected the restrictions on social mobility imposed by aristocratic societies in Europe. By rewarding those who strive for and produce results, the United States has flourished into a nation the rest of the world looks to as a model of freedom and wealth. With few exceptions, our nation has made it possible for every American to achieve his or her goals and dreams. After all, this is why people from all over the world continue to immigrate to the United States. They recognize the educational opportunities offered to each child who attends school in America and they realize the positive economic results of those opportunities. It's as simple as this: *Hard work pays off.* We see this every day in the successful corporations started by individual entrepreneurs like Bill Gates, Steve Jobs, and Warren Buffett. They stand on the shoulders of Ford, Carnegie, and Rockefeller.

If the United States is going to maintain its status as world leader, our schools must continue to emphasize academic achievement and foster citizens who have the drive and energy to dominate the global economy. This requires schools to uphold rigorous academic standards and accountability. We cannot afford to continue to watch other nations increase the mathematic and scientific achievement of their students while many of our students continue to struggle with the basics. After all, what has made our nation great, other than our collective desire to be the best?

Of course some students are not achieving academically but programs are in place to address poverty, disability, and other disadvantages. Why, then, do liberals complain about safety nets and welfare programs? Congress has enacted legislation that offers incentives to districts that raise student achievement, particularly in poor and urban school districts. Additional funds have been allocated to improve schools that cannot meet achievement standards. In addition, special education spends up to three times more money per pupil than is given to students without disabilities.

With few exceptions, disadvantaged students have every opportunity for social mobility, but most of them want life handed to them on a plate, as if their country owes them a living. Bottom line? It all boils down to whether or not they have the motivation to do what it takes to achieve. Personal responsibility and individual accountability are key to success in our great "land of opportunity."

The Importance of Talent and Motivation

We strongly believe that today's schools must reward talent, support the drive to excel, and facilitate the achievement of our most capable students. Over fifty years ago, the national emphasis on science and math education in the post-Sputnik era set us apart from other nations and made it possible for the scientific and economic advances that reinforced the United States' position as a world leader. To keep our position, the country has to prioritize the advantages of students who demonstrate the drive and ability to be our future leaders. Some might argue that such advantages create inequity, yet this argument ignores the fact that everyone has an equal opportunity to work toward their "American Dream."

Too often, we hear liberals complaining about problems in urban schools and the need for broad scale educational reform. We agree that there are social problems but believe that schools alone cannot solve the problems. Communities and families have to be responsible for finding solutions. However, we do have ideas for maintaining and continuously increasing educational achievement. For example, we support legislation that holds schools accountable for student achievement and provides incentives to reward teachers and schools that meet achievement goals. Unfortunately, there is only so much that can be done because, in the end, some families value education and others do not. Some families value hard work and others do not. Some students are more capable than others and some are not. Those who can achieve should be given the opportunity to do so. When they achieve, they are rewarded with everything that comes with the fruits of their labor. Those who can't should be provided with vocational education so that they do not become burdens to society. For the few who will not be able to contribute to society, the welfare system provides a good safety net. However, to avoid reliance on welfare, we must contain its costs by restricting eligibility to the least capable of contributing to society and monitor those who receive assistance. I don't want boatloads of recent immigrants sponging off us—or using government money to buy lottery tickets.

Differences, Harms, and Wrongs

Rather than focusing on maintaining our nation's global standing, there are those who tend to point out our problems and complain about the solutions we offer. For example, they want to water down what's taught with "culturally sensitive pedagogy" and other curriculum modifications that take ways from the established, traditional canon of knowledge, a canon that has proven itself throughout our history. This position neglects the fallout when curriculum veers away from tried and true rigorous academics toward a soft curriculum of relative cultural values in which anything goes. Nor does it recognize the importance of standards—on a national level—that serve as clear guides for instruction and assessment. Rather than leaving curriculum decisions to teachers, many of whom are ill equipped to make important decisions about content, standards give important guidelines about what is important to know and do in America.

We hear a lot about students who are "different"; disabled students, at risk students, immigrant students, and so on. People seem to think that we're one big melting pot and everyone should be in classrooms together. We encourage tolerance in school, but that does not mean schools should reject specific educational programs designed for particular purposes. We believe it is important to consider how schools can maintain rigorous academic standards while also meeting the needs of students who cannot achieve high standards. Special classes are crucial for students who don't have the academic skills or background knowledge to succeed in general education. The intentional creation of heterogeneous classrooms in which students have widely divergent achievement levels distracts general education teachers from their primary responsibility of facilitating academic achievement and preparing students for a productive adult life.

Liberals often resist wholesale any innovative educational models designed to foster achievement—such as charter schools, vouchers, and even the concept of gifted education! They argue that such models ignore the underlying social ills that *create* achievement problems. On the contrary, their position ignores the long-term, large-scale *consequences* of low achievement that we are attempting to prevent. It is easy to criticize, but it's difficult to propose real solutions. More importantly, we are impatient with the critics who resist solutions based on what has been proven to work through scientifically based research. The intrinsic motivations of the market-driven system are the answers to unsuccessful schools. Families rightfully demand quality. It's as simple as this: Schools that provide a quality education will thrive while the rest will fail.

The Antidotes: High Standards, Accountability, Teacher Quality

According to liberals, the solution to the problems in schools is large-scale educational reform that would send a flood of fiscal resources into poor and minority schools. They refer to this as providing equal opportunity. Unfortunately, they neglect to consider the fact that increasing funds to schools serving poor children actually assures very little. It does not improve teacher quality, guarantee academic rigor, or hold districts accountable for results. We propose that these three goals—high standards, accountability, and teacher quality—should be the collective focus of our efforts.

High Standards. What are high standards and why do we need them? We believe high standards primarily consist of expectations about academic achievement. Secondarily, they entail standards of conduct and productivity. Both kinds of standards require conditions that are conducive to them. High standards of achievement require clear, rigorous expectations. Such expectations already exist in each state's curriculum standards and are clarified in the Common Core State Standards that provide a consistent, clear understanding of what students are expected to learn. The question we ask is whether or not these standards actually are applied to all students. Are all students expected to achieve or are some students exempted? Some schools are too lax about whether students speak Standard English when they graduate. Many students are passed along year after year and end up graduating without the literacy skills needed to function in the twenty-first century. For too long, schools have allowed some students to fail, and of course, this is unacceptable to us.

Standards of conduct and productivity are related to achievement. Classrooms need to be managed in ways that expect appropriate group behavior and encourage productive use of time. For example, while we recognize the importance of the arts and physical education, we also know priorities must be placed upon basic skills and content knowledge. So we expect schools to prioritize those subjects that provide students with the skills needed for the adult world of work, namely reading, language arts, and mathematics in the elementary school, and subject matter areas in the secondary school.

To achieve high standards, we must ask about the conditions under which teachers are expected to teach. Are their classrooms filled with students who need too much individual attention and who cannot work by themselves or in large groups? Do these students detract from the time and energy teachers must devote to providing a rigorous curriculum for students who can and should be in the general education classroom? Are families and community members supporting or undermining the work of schools and teachers? While we believe that teachers are one of the most important factors in achieving high standards, we also see the necessity of prioritizing the environment in which they work to make it manageable for them.

Accountability. Accountability calls for public knowledge of how schools are performing academically and consequences—positive or negative—tied to the results. We have established numerous ways of communicating results to the public, including published reports of each school's annual progress. Each school and district provides the public with key information needed for making decisions about school choice. In fact, giving parents choice over where their children attend school, including home schooling, has been a hallmark of our position. When schools are failing, governmental intervention can be used to develop systemic correction and give parents options. Additional funding and oversight can be provided. Some schools must be closed if they have been given additional support and are still unable to improve. It's the survival of the fittest. These market-based solutions are the tried and true way of reforming education.

We also call for individual accountability. Teacher and principal performance must reflect the priorities that lead to achievement. Teachers whose students are under-performing academically should be identified and must be required to improve. In order to do this, we should be clear about which teachers are responsible for which students. Remembering that special education teachers are trained to work with disabled students, schools should carefully consider whether and when to integrate them into general education classrooms. Unfortunately that doesn't clear up the problem of "at risk" students and students who don't speak English. Who should be responsible for them? We also need to remember that some students are intrinsically motivated to excel while others require extrinsic motivation.

Teacher Quality. We cannot have high standards and accountability without emphasizing teacher quality. A great deal of attention is often given to students who are not motivated. This is usually done at the expense of the most capable students. We believe that quality teachers pay close attention to those students who exhibit high ability and motivation to excel. After all, these students are our future "movers and shakers" in

Case 2: "Ableism at Forest Run"

Ableism? When did that new word get invented? While we don't agree with Shelly's characterization of Jesse as a flatliner, we wonder when the liberals will stop inventing new victims. Of course Shelly is concerned about Jesse's achievement. She's responsible for his learning and for the progress of her entire class. We would expect her to refer any struggling student to the appropriate school professionals. We are also concerned with Judith's response. She should be recommending lessons that get at learning standards, not designing activities that correct other teachers' thinking. Furthermore, there seems to be an implicit assumption that standardized testing is wrong or bad for students. We don't advocate standardized tests as the only way to assess achievement. But standardized testing does have its benefits, particularly when assessing students on a large-scale basis. This case demonstrates much that is wrong with liberal sensibilities by emphasizing values and emotions over academic achievement.

Case 3: "Race, Place, and the Search for Solutions"

The problems in this school are typical for many urban schools. We're glad to see the principal's efforts to gain parent participation. We're also glad to see a local journalist keeping educational issues in the news. As to the question of whether or not special education will help solve the problems in this school, we say "maybe." Yet we are concerned about the national trend to increase the number of students eligible for special education. That is a financially extravagant way to solve school-wide problems. The U.S. Department of Education has known about the national achievement gap for decades, so we can't be sure that any single-school solution will be sufficient. Our proposals for high standards, accountability, and teacher quality would help here. So would our recommendation that schools stop focusing on racial differences and start focusing on the high academic achievement needed to maintain our country's position in the global economy. Nothing is mentioned about teacher quality at CVHS. We would want to examine that issue as well as whether or not the community is willing to follow through with solutions that involve time and money. Or is this community interested in government spending to solve its problems?

Case 4: *"Special* Educator?"

This case speaks directly to the antidotes we propose. Martin does seem to be a bit inflexible and we attribute some of that to his inexperience. Yet Martin's intense focus on content appeals to us in light of our interest in high standards. We admire his colleagues' attempts to help him adjust his teaching strategies and expectations but we wonder about how far Martin should go with these. We support his concern about watering down the curriculum. Why, in fact, is the special education teacher in the building if she's not providing direct service to students?

Instead of urging Martin to adjust his high standards and water down the curriculum, we recommend that he and his colleagues evaluate whether school resources are being used effectively. Why, in fact, are so many special education students in Martin's classroom? Are the special education students getting the assistance they need from the special education department? Does Martin have opportunities to observe and interact with high quality teachers in his own subject area? Are the parents of his students held accountable for academically supporting their children at home? How does the school support teachers like Martin who have high expectations and intend to hold students accountable?

A "LIBERAL-PROGRESSIVE VIEW": CELEBRATING DIVERSITY, CREATING EQUITY

Introduction

The concept of the American Dream is central to our culture. The idea of living a life unfettered by the circumstances of birth, and with the possibility of reaching for the stars to make anything happen, has a universal appeal. It provides promise and hope to millions of people born within the US and countless others from around the world who wish to immigrate here. There are examples all around of "self-made men" (and women), individuals who overcame enormous odds making it from rags-to-riches in this "land of opportunity." There's also a tacit belief that all it takes to "make it" is personal drive, a strong work ethic, and the will to succeed. U.S. history prominently features "rugged individualism" as a national characteristic in both leading figures and everyday people. The notion of everyone "pulling themselves up by their bootstraps" is compatible with enculturating citizens as fiercely independent individuals who need minimal governmental support.

Of course we cannot deny some elements of truth within the American Dream. It serves to inspire and motivate people, many of whom follow its trajectory toward achieving their dreams (and over time, perhaps a modified version of them). However, to achieve the American Dream ignores the reality of discrimination within the US, and the barriers erected—physical, psychological, social, emotional, and *academic*—by that discrimination. Since its inception, our country has valued some groups over others. The often-cited phrase "All men are created equal" from the U.S. Declaration of Independence is deceptive. During that time, it signified all wealthy, White, males—actually the *elite* within society. It did not include women, the working class and poor people, enslaved African Americans, other people of color, or immigrants.

Although the ideals of freedom and equality continue to resonate throughout our culture, great inequalities persist. For example, even today some social groups continue to remain an underclass, having few resources, with little access to all that society has to offer. The majority of people with disabilities fall into this category—facing discrimination in employment and housing, with limited means of transportation and social possibilities. In sum, equal opportunities are severely curtailed.

The Importance of Equal Opportunity

Education is often seen as the great equalizer that allows all citizens an opportunity to work, study, grow, and follow their dreams in a country that self-defines as a place where "dreams come true." Schools are perceived as institutions that—among other things—prepare students for further education and/or the workforce. However, we have to call into question to what degree schools actually can create a level playing field for all citizens. There are *huge* discrepancies between districts as well as among schools within a single district.

Without wishing to oversimplify, some schools have stable leadership, highly qualified and certified teachers, state of the art technology, an innovative contemporary curriculum, and modern facilities. In contrast, other schools have rotating leadership, unqualified and temporarily certified teachers, outdated or minimal technology, a curriculum limited by outdated materials, and old facilities. Oftentimes, these discrepancies can be characterized by an urban-suburban divide or rural-suburban divide. It is also more likely that it reflects a White community vs. a community mostly comprised of people of color.

Within both "types" of school at either end of this continuum, and all other schools that fall somewhere between these fairly common extremes, students with disabilities must navigate a playing field that is filled with contradictions and paradoxes. For example, while they are guaranteed a free and appropriate education by law, the placement and quality of experience can vary dramatically according to disability *and* race *and* social class. Middle-class White parents are more likely to have their child placed in a "good" school (i.e. matching the descriptors above) or even a private school at public expense. In addition, the child may receive more services (physical therapy, speech and language, one-on-one attention in resource room) and accommodations (use of a laptop, extended time) than their poorer counterpart, likely a parent of color. Instead, the poor counterpart will have more chance of attending a "bad" school, receiving fewer services and accommodations, and not knowing about options.

These realities demonstrate the importance of striving to level the playing field where K-12 education is supported across all neighborhoods, in all areas, across the country. The situation speaks to providing access to equal resources for all children, including a push toward academic rigor and ultimately, increased possibilities for engaging in post-secondary education. It also requires an infusion of financial and personnel resources to update the infrastructure of many schools that will, in turn, make higher education possible for any qualified student, regardless of family's income and educational background.

Conservatives like to claim that government intervention is unnecessary for solving the problems confronting education. They say, "Let the people decide how to run their schools," and "Schools should be a reflection of the values of the local community." If this is the case, we must ask: Who's going to watch out for those who have no voice? Who's going to make sure that equality of opportunity exists across the board? We believe that local communities should be concerned about discrimination against its disabled citizens, but government has a responsibility and must monitor these instances as well. It has been said that you can tell a lot about a society by the way it treats its most vulnerable citizens. We believe this is especially true when it comes to disability in education. After all, America is strongest when all Americans have a fair chance at opportunities to achieve success and can contribute to society.

Differences, Harms, and Wrongs

As our society becomes more diverse, schools are faced with increasing challenges in meeting the educational needs of all students. When we talk about diversity we are not just talking about race, ethnicity, gender, or sexual orientation. Disability is one aspect of diversity, yet we observe that many schools do not recognize it as such. When any kind of diversity is neglected, minimized, or simply ignored, students who represent that specific form of diversity can become isolated and stigmatized. We see this happening to disabled students who are often typically characterized as a "problem," "inconvenience," or "challenge" because they may not fit the school mold they are expected to fit into.

It is problematic that society in general—and this includes schools—has less tolerance for natural human differences that we have come to characterize as disabilities than for its able-bodied citizens. Fear of the unknown is deep. Fear of disability is also deep. Inadequate experience and erroneous knowledge can cause discomfort, panic, and rejection. Initial responses of teachers such as "I don't know how to . . .," "I can't do it . . .," "This is really for an expert . . .," "I have not been trained . . .," and so on, are common. Related to this, is the idea of changing how we plan for, assess, teach, engage, evaluate, and integrate all students into classroom culture. The realization of one size does *not* fit all can initially be intimidating to teachers, who have to shift their preconceived notions of what teaching is, and how it looks in action.

Another aspect of teaching students with disabilities that raises questions is the simple notion of "What's fair?" Conservatives sometimes characterize people with disabilities as "a special interest group" and interpret special needs as "special deals" that give students with disabilities an unfair advantage over others. For example, having additional time for examinations, using different formats (e.g. oral vs. written), use of technology, etc. may initially create uncomfortable situations in classrooms when other students do not have these. In a way, teachers see accommodations and other considerations as a form of affirmative action that can detract from, and be unfair to, academically stronger students.

The Antidotes: Celebrating Diversity, Creating Opportunity, and Addressing Fairness

The issues outlined above reflect some of the complexities involved when schools grapple with how to best understand and teach students with disabilities within what is already a diverse student body. We would like to point out what is perhaps obvious to some readers already, that disability cuts across all of the other forms of diversity—including social class, gender, race, ethnicity, nationality, sexual orientation, second language learners, and so on. We view this as further evidence that issues of disability must be recognized as integral to understanding diversity among all students. In the following section we propose three broad areas—celebrating diversity, creating opportunity, and addressing fairness—to help counter discrimination against students with disabilities, and promote greater equity within classrooms.

Celebrating Diversity. Although much progress has been made in regard to providing access to general education for students with disabilities, and to society in general for people with disabilities, there is still a long way to go. What can be gained from integrating disability into the plethora of differences that already exist? Because children with disabilities are subjected to stigmatizing practices and associations, we urge teachers to "work against the grain," and understand disability not primarily as a negative attribute, but rather as one aspect of a child's identity that can come to determine that child's experience in school. Much can be done to dispel the discomfort of students with (and without) disabilities if disability is integral as part of content, curriculum, and discussions. This can take many forms, ranging from the explicit teaching of disability in general, or a specific disability, such as the ones students in class may have. In the documentary *Including Samuel* (Habib, 2008), Samuel's parents variously explain to 1st graders the use of his motorized wheelchair, communication board, ways in which he is fed, and how he takes his medicine. Likewise, in the film *I Have Tourette's but Tourette's Doesn't Have Me* (Kent, 1996), a middle school student explains to his classmates about his condition—and encourages them to ask questions. In turn, they respond with genuine curiosity and respectful inquiries.

These examples serve to demystify specific disabilities in ways that "make sense" to students, and diminish any potential fears they may have. Addressing "disability etiquette," the do's and don'ts of engaging with people who have a variety of conditions is another worthwhile area to address, precisely to dispel myths and remove taboos. Over the past few decades, much has been written in terms of ways of working toward a classroom in which "Everybody Belongs" (A. Shapiro, 1999). In addition, there are many children's books featuring progressive portrayals of protagonists with disabilities that can be integrated into classroom libraries as part of a multicultural curriculum (see, for example, Bang, 2004, Haddon, 2003, and Levine, 1999). That said, educators must also be vigilant of representations of disabilities that reinforce stereotypes or emphasize inabilities (Ayala, 1999).

Creating Opportunity. Teaching a classroom of diverse students is both challenging and rewarding. Teachers must take into consideration students who have physical, cognitive, behavioral, and sensory impairments as they create their curriculum and design lessons. As a result, teachers become more nuanced planners, flexible in their approach, cultivating a general disposition toward accommodating all students. Another helpful way for teachers to think about this challenge is through the lens of "access." In other words, teachers aim to provide access through a variety of means for all students to "enter and participate within" their lesson.

In brief, all aspects of the lesson are designed to connect with students. For example, creating links to a student's prior knowledge helps to connect them to the current content being taught. Providing opportunities for students to reach their next level of development through a series of interrelated questions and tasks—while being supported by the teacher—helps them grow academically, socially, and emotionally. Varying the format between individual work, student partners, triads, group work, and whole class instruction facilitates learning for all students who learn better in particular ways.

What teachers are often surprised to find out is that not only *can* they provide different tasks for students to do—but they *should* do so, according to those students' needs. Given the diversity within classrooms and our earlier discussion of how one size cannot fit all, over the past decade or more, the notion of differentiated instruction has gained prominence. The work of Carol Ann Tomlinson (1999, 2001) in particular has guided educators to see differentiating aspects of their teaching to have a systematic way of instructing all students. Thus, being able to differentiate the content (what is being taught), the process (how it is being taught), and the product (how learning is demonstrated) provides ways to connect with, and engage students, in learning. Differentiation can also be used based upon other factors such as students' readiness, interests, and learning profile. This, we know, is a topic of huge importance—and beyond the page lengths allowed in this slim volume—so we do encourage you to read further in this area.

Addressing Fairness. "What is fair?" is, fittingly, a fair question. Of course who gets to decide what is fair and the criteria used to determine that decision opens us all up to different conceptualizations of fairness. The two previously discussed areas of accepting, representing, and celebrating diversity, along with creating opportunities to access the curriculum are both pertinent to the related realm of fairness. How should teachers respond when student A sees student B doing something that student A is not allowed to do, such as take the weekly exam in another format? Complete five problems instead of ten? Dictate responses rather than write them? What if, in a co-teaching situation, the general educator tends to be more conservative in his or her approach and does not like the idea of having a different exam for some students with IEPs? A different in-class academic task? A different format in assessing the knowledge of one student?

Collaborating teachers must set time aside so they can discuss all issues pertaining to their classroom, including why particular students need certain accommodations and modifications—some of which they're entitled to by law. Co-teachers can actively work together in planning units and lessons, as well as constantly debrief about the successes and challenges of teaching recent lessons. Part of their ongoing conversations must be around "what is fair" for each student in their class, including which students, with and without IEPs.

Teachers can be open with their classes about their philosophy and policy of providing different students with various ways of engaging in tasks, providing evidence of learning, and being assessed. Teaching about different understandings of fairness to students is essential, as they can shift according to circumstances. In her paraphrasing of the work on fairness by Deutsch (1975), Ann Welch (2000) describes three forms of "fair" that can be appropriate in some situations.

(a) *Equality.* "There are times when it is fair to treat everyone the same way. Every citizen gets a vote. Every child gets a teacher" (p. 36). She also notes that schools would look quite different if every child had safe housing, healthy food, supportive relationships at home, and qualified teachers.

(b) *Equity.* "There are also times when it is fair to make rewards proportionate to input. In this case, we celebrate those who excel. If everyone has an equal opportunity to participate, those who perform well should be rewarded" (p. 36). Welch reminds us that this definition exemplifies that the best candidate should get the job, regardless of gender, race, or disability. In terms of school, we must teach all children to do math, but we recognize the most gifted mathematician.

(c) *Need.* "The third definition of fairness is need. Wheelchair ramps, free lunches, and special education are provided not to everyone (equality) or to the best (equity), but to those who need them the most" (p. 36). Within a classroom, this principle may be applied to everything from the length of an assignment to the number of bathroom breaks allowed.

In sum, different meanings of fairness are applicable to various situations, and teachers can benefit from understanding and utilizing all three of these meanings, as well as explicitly discussing them with their students.

COMMENTS AND QUESTIONS

"The Liberal View and You"

General Questions

1   With which aspects of this argument did you agree and why?

2   With which aspects did you disagree and why?

3   How did this public argument change or reinforce your ideas about what counts as "liberal"?

Specific Questions

1   The liberal view takes a strong position on the importance of recognizing existing inequities and creating ways in which the playing field is made even. What are some potential consequences with this focus? What kind of student does it favor? What might be some assumptions underlying this focus in relation to students with disabilities?

2   Considering the antidote of celebrating disability as diversity, what are some potential problems with the way it is framed in the liberal view? For example, who does this framing favor and why?

Having explored the focus on "Creating Equal Opportunity," we now take a look at each of the four cases, considering them within the framework of the liberal view.

Case 1: "Inclusion Tension"

This case reveals the divide among both administrators and teachers toward including students with disabilities. The principal urges his faculty

to see inclusion as a philosophy that undergirds all decisions about instruction and student placement. He sees inclusion as a way to increase more
equal opportunities, and at the same time, be flexible toward students with
disabilities who do not fit the mold yet need to participate in mandated
examinations. The "tensions," in part, arise from considering how best to
operationalize inclusive practices when they are rooted within a philosophy that appears to sometimes go against the competing demand of
educational reform. Educators feel "caught in the crossfire" between
providing equal opportunities to all students, while at the same time working within a system that is based upon competition that reinforces
individualism.

"Inclusion Tension" raises important questions about choice, and the
important roles that teachers play in influencing students who are labeled
disabled and where they receive their education. A Liberal-Progressive
response first gives the benefit of any doubt about inclusion on the side
of students, as we recognize disability as a form of human diversity
akin to others. Since our country is built upon the premise of equality, it
would be unfair, indeed un-American, to disempower a portion of the
population. Furthermore, if test scores (especially fear of poor results)
are the singular overarching reason for decision-making, then they are
being used at the expense of a historically disenfranchised group. It is an
unfortunate situation for teachers to be caught in the middle of such
tensions caused by education policies, but they must see their way clear to
what's morally right and that includes working with all of the citizens of
this country.

Case 2: "Ableism at Forest Run"

Ableism. We're glad that a word is being used to describe what we have
all seen and heard many times—but couldn't put our finger on it. Now
we can name it for what it is—overt discrimination against people with
disabilities that occurs in both obvious and subtle ways. Unfortunately,
many special educators who are basically well intentioned "good
people" are subject to the onslaught of stereotypes and misinformation
about disabilities and "take up" all of the negative, deficit-based understandings that saturate the media and, sadly, most of the field's textbooks (Brantlinger, 2006). Shelly's interpretation of Jesse exemplifies
this phenomenon, and she automatically pigeonholes Jesse, focusing
on what he can't do, how he looks, and therefore what to expect from
him.

In contrast, Judith is far more questioning of "norms" and "standards" that can be used *against* children. Judith's reflective disposition leads her to challenge stereotypes around disability, stigmatization, and isolation within communities. She does this with children in her classroom, but is more hesitant to engage Shelly, and other teachers in her school, who dismiss students that transfer from a different district as unable to "catch up." This case reveals how structural inequalities within society "stick" to certain children, and teachers are in the position of either shrugging off the situation with "That's the way it is," or actively working toward seeing and understanding children's individual needs that can be addressed through differentiation, flexible approaches to instruction, and an acceptance of diversity. Ironically Judith, the general educator, is the role model in this case as she works against disability stereotypes, predispositions, and is intent upon creating a classroom that engages in issues around diversity and fairness.

Case 3: "Race, Place, and the Search for Solutions"

Does a student have to be labeled disabled in order to receive the academic support he or she needs? This has been the case over the past few decades and likely explains, at least in part, why so many children of color and English Language Learners from chronically underfunded and under supported school districts are categorized as disabled (Artiles, Rueda, Salazar, & Higareda, 2002). In recalling previous points made about "fairness" within classrooms, what about fairness within schools across the country? Likewise, in recalling previous comments made about the importance of academic standards, what about having standards for equal resources to schools nationwide? Very few people would disagree with providing one-on-one support for students who need that support, but legally *disabling* them to receive support is wrong on so many levels.

Instead of a "band-aid" approach of providing more special educators to help a targeted group of children to make better scores (and become disabled in the process), a liberal-progressive view argues for restructuring funding mechanisms, taxes, and zoning laws so that all schools receive what they need to help them prepare students to meet the standards. After all, individualized tutoring can be provided without disability labels. It's time for the U.S. policy makers to be honest in recognizing that our entrenched racial inequalities are still evident across the nation, and this is no more obvious than in public schools and the neighborhoods they serve.

Case 4: *"Special* Educator?"

All of us who went into teaching did so with certain expectations. To a large degree, many of us expected that the kids would sit straight up, pay attention, be fascinated by our presentations, ask thoughtful questions, be polite, interested, and so on. In some ways we all have an idealized classroom living in our mind's eye, a desirable image of US ourselves leading world peace within four walls. However, all of who went into teaching learned quickly to shift our impressions, expectations, and even some hitherto firm beliefs when we stood in front of students who did not match this idealized, imaginary portrayal. These shifts helped us to adapt to working with actual children and youth who we may never have been exposed to, or interacted with, before. Surprisingly, content matter we loved did not quite have the same effect on our students, and we learned to motivate, engage, and challenge students in ways that honored their current knowledge, experiences, and questions. This is a different skill set than usually taught in university courses. So, Martin's case is really not unique—as all new teachers enter into a learning curve that makes them rethink what and how they're teaching.

Most liberal progressives will likely argue Martin needs to change before his students can. He must adapt to them—by accepting who they are, including their strengths, limitations, and interests. He must consider these factors when planning lessons, and collaborating with his mentor and the special education teacher. By studying his students and getting to know them, Martin can utilize that information to connect with them in ways they understand, provide opportunities for them to engage in the content, and to demonstrate their knowledge. Resisting or rejecting the diversity of abilities in the room is not realistic. It's in Martin's interests to adapt to student variation—as teaching can and should be a pleasurable experience that pushes students' thinking and expands their knowledge, not an interaction that frustrates both teacher and student.

A "DISABILITY-CENTERED VIEW": ACKNOWLEDGING DIFFERENCE, DECONSTRUCTING NORMALCY

Introduction

The bottom line is this: We expect to be treated as full and equal members of society. No compromises. We are not second-class citizens. We *are* a large minority group that cuts across all races, ethnicities, and age groups.

This does not necessarily unite us, although in the eyes of many—it should. As citizens, we have civil rights, and those rights include attending school and university with *all* of our peers—including those with and without disabilities.

We're tired of being treated like we're abnormal, like there's something wrong with being different. Don't get us wrong, we do not deny our bodily differences and ways in which we move, act, sense, think, and behave. However, our impairments are only one part of who we are, and we're tired of the overemphasis on what we cannot do versus what we can. Schools are a prime example of this detrimental practice in which a disability label comes to define a student's educational identity, including their classroom placement. Widespread ableism surrounds us, but able-bodied people either cannot or choose not to acknowledge it. In fact, one of the many unacknowledged luxuries of able-bodied people is to not have to think about it! Whereas, if a person has a disability, it can impact all aspects of our lives on a daily basis, from where we live and go to school, our degree of access to college, securing a job, dating, and mundane daily tasks such as shopping, taking public transportation, using recreational activities, and being fully integrated within the community.

We need greater access to all aspects of society, and that access begins in schools. There is not a parallel "special" world in which we exist outside of school, so why should there be one inside? If kids don't see other children with disabilities and teachers with disabilities in their classes, how will they ever see them as equals who are different? We're tired of being defined by others within the fields of science, psychology, medicine, and education that view us as "lacking," "not fully human," "disordered," "dysfunctional," "deficit-based." What if the tables were turned and all of our definers were, instead, defined by us as oppressive, wrong, misleading, limited, stereotypic, and self-interested? That's exactly why our mantra is "Nothing about us without us," because the natural differences among us have been characterized in such dehumanizing ways.

The Importance of Rethinking What You Know

When only men wrote the history of women, how were females characterized? The answer is: inferior, less intelligent, weaker, more emotional, less stable, irrational, childlike, unpredictable, and, in comparison to men, unable to participate in all aspects of society. When only people of European descent wrote the history of African Americans, how were Black people characterized? The answer is: inferior, less intelligent, more

people w/ disabilities are being treated like the Blacks were in history emotional, less stable, irrational, childlike, unpredictable, and, in comparison to Whites, unable to participate in all aspects of society. As you can see, a pattern is emerging, so as we ask: When only able-bodied people write the history of disabled people, how are people with disabilities characterized? It should be no surprise that the answers are similar: inferior, less intelligent, less stable, unpredictable, childlike, and, in comparison to able-bodied people, unable to participate in all aspects of society. Along with sexism and racism, ableism is a very potent force that reinforces stereotypes, perpetuates barriers—both physical and attitudinal—and prevents people with disabilities gaining access too, participating in, and contributing to all aspects of society.

The simple notion of who is speaking for whom is very powerful, because in the vast majority of instances, disabled people are not speaking for, or representing, themselves. If this was the case of men defining women, or Whites defining Blacks, there would be an uproar. So we ask: Why is it acceptable for the continuation of people with disabilities to be defined by others? How accurate are those definitions? And, what are the consequences of those definitions when they are circulated throughout all aspects of society?

Differences, Harms, and Wrongs

What disturbs us is how the field of special education is largely built on foundations laid within science, medicine, and psychology. While all of these fields obviously have helped define, cure, and heal many members of society, they also exert a great influence over how we come to understand human differences that become characterized as disabilities. What we're saying here is that differences among us exist, but it is our response to those differences that is most important and reveals our dispositions toward other humans. As mentioned earlier in this book, special education is predicated on difference being interpreted as dysfunction, disorder, deficit, something that needs to be cured, fixed, or restored to normalcy. We contend that this way of thinking, so prevalent in special educational research and college textbooks, is dangerous, damaging, and reductive because it pathologizes human differences that are actually quite normal within nature, and this leads those pathologized to believe they are actually inferior to "normal" people (Rodis, Garrod, & Boscardin, 2001).

Schools of education prepare teachers to work in schools, and part of this training is engagement with traditional textbooks that portray children with disabled children in ways that emphasize their "deficits" as opposed to understanding them in the holistic context of their lives. In addition, special educators are viewed as the "experts" in dealing with such deficits, reinforcing the split between what constitutes general and special— making an artificial divide appear real: two types of children need two types of teachers. Public school systems also reinforce this divide in terms of their structures—separate departments, rooms, floors, offices, etc. Within the official school curriculum, traditional representations of disability are reinforced at every turn. For example the "classic" texts within English Language Arts serve to reinforce reactions of pity (*The Glass Menagerie*), charity (*A Christmas Carol*), revulsion (*Hunchback of Notre Dame*), fear (*Of Mice and Men*), evil (*Richard III*), and occasional awe (*The Miracle Worker*). This list symbolizes representation within other fields such as film, TV, cartoons, drama, etc., in which people with disabilities are never a three-dimensional character, but instead almost always serve to symbolize negativity. We would like to ask you: Can you name positive examples of representing disability as part of human diversity? In turn, if you can, we are delighted; if you can't, we're not surprised.

Conservatives will likely dismiss our claims of being ignored, excluded, and misrepresented in schools and society as evidence of a self-serving special-interest agenda that deflects from important issues, threatens to lower standards, and overextend already limited resources. Liberal progressives will likely see much of what we say is true, and will join ranks in providing support, but may find us a bit too radical when we advocate for *all* children to be included. After all, we are eager to see massive, widespread change toward creating greater access to all aspects of society for disabled people, and that includes schools.

The Antidotes: Challenging Normalcy, Diversifying the Curriculum, and Advocating for Activism

We have made some progress since the passage of legislation to protect the rights of individuals with disabilities and to guarantee a free and "appropriate" public school education. However, people with disabilities are still "open game" for insults and jokes, and are relentlessly stereotyped in all areas of society while being denied the right to participate in all aspects of that society. To counter limited expectations, redress inaccurate portrayals, and challenge the definitions of disability by "experts" (including special educators), people with disabilities have asserted themselves in ways that "talk back" to mainstream ways. Three of the many areas in which they have been successful can be described as challenging (by deconstructing) the notion of normalcy, revising curricula consisting of inaccurate portrayals, and mobilizing to politically engage organizations, institutions, and media about their limited and oftentimes damaging understandings of disability while offering alternatives.

Challenging Normalcy. The concept of "normal" is something that we take for granted without really questioning where it comes from, or how it's used, where, when, and by whom. In brief, the sugar-coated euphemism of "special" education actually represents students who are *disabled*—but that particular word sounds too harsh or stigmatizing or both. What's even harsher and more stigmatizing is the word "abnormal," yet this is exactly what children with disabilities are considered. Deviations from the norm are aberrations that schools seek to fix, remediate, redress, and/or contain. But special education has not "fixed" children, and nor should it seek to. Many of its methods are questionable, including exclusion, an overemphasis on wholesale rote drill of skills, memorization, and overemphasis on behavioral techniques such as applied behavioral analysis, that can easily deaden the dynamic nature of learning. The results of special education have also proven ineffective on many fronts, including a high drop-out rate, poor graduation statistics, unemployment and underemployment, and a link to crime and prison (Karagiannis, 2000).

A more accurate way of describing how children with disabilities, say, dyslexia, Learning Disability, or Behavior Disorder are not "fixed" or do not "overcome" their condition is to state that they learn to *manage* how their bodies interact with their environments. Likewise, many self-advocates with autism do not want a cure for autism, because they are happy with who they are and how they function in the world (Broderick & Ne'eman, 2008). Children who don't fit the mold of normalcy serve the purpose of calling to our attention that one size does not, will not, cannot, and should not fit all students. More importantly, it is critical for all educators to be aware of ways in which schools and educational practices actively construct what is considered normal—be it grade expectations of academic performance, social and emotional "milestones," behavioral standards, formal assessments, or school-based tests. Students who fall outside of the arbitrarily drawn, culturally determined, and fluctuating line of normalcy need to understand ways in which to reject categorizations that diminish their status simply because their body functions in ways that are not always compatible with the expectations demanded within a school environment.

Diversifying the Curriculum. One of the ways in which to challenge existing notions of normalcy is by asserting *the normalcy of difference* throughout the curriculum at both K-12 and college levels (particularly within teacher education programs). If, as some scholars have argued, disability is seen as a "minority" status within the field of multiculturalism, then it should be represented in all manner of materials, from books in classroom libraries to teacher "read alouds," from past immigration policies to the Holocaust, from character studies in literature to historical figures ranging from presidents (FDR) to artists (Frida Kahlo). The study of discrimination in previous and current times should be an integral part of the curriculum, as well as the mobilization of people with disabilities and their allies to form the Disability Rights Movement. Explicitly teaching about attitudes and physical barriers helps children recognize when they encounter them.

Another way of challenging normalcy is to reduce ableism within the classroom. Something that is within reach of every teacher is to focus on language. Most people are unaware of ways in which everyday language conveys "put downs" of people with disabilities via expressions such as "that's lame," "that's dumb," "that's retarded." Each one of these, along with commonplace expressions such as "the blind leading the blind," "Are you deaf?," "Can't you see?," and so on, can be considered "micro-aggressions" that repeatedly target people with disabilities. Students can discuss the power of language and ways in which it impacts how we (mis) understand and (re)value other humans.

Although much more could be written here on creating class projects about disability awareness, studying stereotyping, analyzing news stories, staging film festivals, making connections between disability and inventions (Bell's telephone) and innovations (Monet's painting techniques), and so on, the most important aspect of changing the curriculum is featuring the voices of people with disabilities themselves. This should be done at both the school level, as well as the college level, particularly in teacher education programs, otherwise special education texts typically only provide medicalized portrayals of and checklists of "symptoms" denoting "what's wrong" with children.

Advocating Activism. If there continues to be silence around disability it will almost certainly perpetuate shame and stigmatization. In many ways, if children (and adults) who have been categorized as disabled can explain to others what it means to be labeled, what they are good at, and what they have difficulty with, they are self-advocating. In classrooms, the sole emphasis on competition should be on collaboration and cooperation where a few always win and the majority lose; we believe that interdependence is more meaningful than independence.

For those with an invisible disability, the act of "coming out" as disabled is a form of self-advocacy because it gives the person an opportunity to make his or her presence felt. So, when instances of ableism inevitably arise, the disabled person can call attention to them, making them visible to people who are usually unaware. Thus, shifting from "the disability closet" that perpetuates disempowerment, to "coming out" with view to being vocal, to represent a group, to articulate instances of injustice and propose potential solutions within everyday occurrences, signifies a change in power dynamics. Being "out" means we operate from a position of power.

Allies of people with disabilities can also be advocates in that they ensure children with disabilities have the same opportunities in schools as non-disabled students to participate in all aspects of school life—including assemblies, sports events, class trips, after school clubs, and group projects. As classroom situations arise that pertain to disabilities as human differences, educators should be willing to take them "head on," and "in their stride," in order to show their commitment to changing attitudes and removing barriers.

COMMENTS AND QUESTIONS

"The Disability-Centered View and You"

General Questions

1 With which aspects of this argument did you agree and why?

2 With which aspects did you disagree and why?

3 How did this public argument change or reinforce your ideas about what counts as "disability-centered"?

Specific Questions

1 The disability-centered view takes a strong position on the importance of recognizing privileging the perspectives of people with disabilities. What are some potential consequences with this focus? What kind of student does it favor? What might be some assumptions underlying this focus in relation to students with disabilities?

2 Considering the antidotes of challenging normalcy, diversifying the curriculum, and advocating for activism, what are some potential

problems with the way it is framed in the disability-centered view? For example, who does this framing favor and why?

Having explored the focus on "Acknowledging Difference, Deconstructing Normalcy," we now take a look at each of the four cases, considering them within the framework of the disability-centered view.

Case 1: "Inclusion Tension"

Although test scores are important, children are more important. While it is important that everyone "achieves," it is more important for everyone to belong. Teachers have an incredibly demanding job juggling so many things that, for some, inclusion can feel like "the straw that broke the camel's back." We respectfully recognize that one person cannot do everything in an inclusive classroom. That's why other supports and teaching arrangements can and must be made—such as co-planning curriculum with peers, team teaching, collaborating with paraprofessionals (and other support personnel), and participating in professional development to prepare and sustain inclusion models. What's often done in the name of inclusion is irresponsible and, to be blunt, it is *not* inclusion if supports guaranteed by law are not in place.

We understand all of the complexities above when it comes to implementing inclusive practices throughout a school, but the alternative of practicing exclusion is simply untenable. What is at stake here, and is the elephant in the room, are the civil rights of our young disabled citizens. Teachers should not be in a position to choose who they want in their classrooms. They are paid to teach the general public—and that includes children with disabilities. On the other hand, the state's push for higher standards for all must factor in how many students with disabilities take the required exams and how these are weighted or taken into consideration, so that schools are not penaliz:d and people lose jobs. Otherwise, history will repeat itself and schools will create barriers to prevent students with disabilities from gaining access. After all, what is the incentive for administrators to support disabled students when so much is at stake?

Case 2: "Ableism at Forest Run"

Shelly exemplifies many special educators. She is dedicated to helping her students and willing to collaborate with general educators. However, her disposition toward difference is problematic as it is entrenched in deficit-based models so prevalent within special education teacher training programs. Describing a child as a "flatliner" is not meant to be offensive, but it is because it reveals her personal assessment of Jesse as unable to show any discernible growth or progress. There is such an irony to disabled people that special educators unwittingly demonstrate all kinds of ableist views, although we do understand that the profession enculturates teachers to think in this way.

Judith, it strikes us, has a healthier, more holistic outlook on what constitutes student diversity. She is mindful of how quick assessments can stereotype children and their abilities, and how teacher judgment plays a significant role in where students are educated—from separate classrooms to within a hierarchy of table arrangements within general education. Judith works against such practices by rejecting the notion that Jesse is a flatliner. Furthermore, she is sensitive to his struggles to fit in and be accepted by peers. Her choice of teaching *Crow Boy*, and the student-centered conversations that ensue, along with children's drawings, provide a forum in which to discuss diversity, difference, and disability. While not naming ableism as the force she is countering, Judith is actually doing so on multiple levels.

Case 3: "Race, Place, and the Search for Solutions"

Increasing the number of special educators to help raise student test scores doesn't make sense. The problems in this situation are too vast and complicated for a singular, simple solution. What this case does reveal is institutional racism in the form of schools within poor communities of color not receiving the level of material support needed. African American and Latino students who are traditionally over-represented in special education are perceived not only deficit-based in disability, but also deficit-based in culture, and deficit-based in language. Once again, this leads us back to ideas of normalcy—standards based on "traditional" norms rooted in White, middle-class, English-only speaking, and ableist values. The school is a microcosm of the country, and until the playing field is evened in terms of community resources, access to employment, and the belief that fairness means providing people what they need—not just telling everyone that they are free and have a fair chance—this situation will not change. To begin with, more resources must be provided to this school.

In addition, the beliefs and attitudes of all community members should be engaged with to further explore what can be done. One or two Parent

Teacher Association meetings in which a variety of opinions are shared is only the start. At these meetings, the role that special education plays in raising test scores can be an ongoing item for discussion, along with ways to best utilize funding earmarked for special education. However, restructuring the school to provide greater access for disabled students to general education classes, and figuring out ways to support all students as they engage with the skills and knowledge required of the curriculum, makes more sense to us than only increasing the number of special education teachers for one-on-one tutoring. Such tutoring should be a service available for all students.

Case 4: *"Special* Educator?"

Martin has an idea in his head about *who* he should be teaching. The reality is that he is teaching youth from the general public—and he needs to accept that. However, as one-third of his students have disabilities, we'd like to point out that this is a large number that is really not in line with good inclusive practices. While a universal formula is not useful in every situation, it makes sense that the number of students with and without disabilities should reflect the ratio within the general population—which is approximately 15% to 20%. That said, we acknowledge that teachers are often placed in less than ideal situations and must make them work as best they can. As a social studies teacher, Martin needs to become aware of disabled students' civil rights to be in his class. At the same time, he needs to adapt toward WHO he is teaching, instead of primarily valuing WHAT he is teaching. This, in and of itself, would signify a greater acceptance of student diversity.

In many ways, Martin's belief that it's not his job to teach disabled students stems from our segregated teacher education programs. Who is "normal" gets to be in general education to participate in the social studies curriculum; who is "abnormal" should be placed elsewhere for a modified version. Instead, we see Martin's job as creating a classroom where everyone "fits." This may mean students participating in different ways, demonstrating knowledge in different ways, and being assessed in different ways. Such a simple and radical idea must be valued more within teacher education programs—as part of a disability-centered curriculum that confronts ableism and challenges longstanding notions of what a normal classroom looks like.

III

A FINAL ARGUMENT, AND SOME SUGGESTIONS AND RESOURCES FOR FURTHER REFLECTION

In this final section we undertake three tasks. First, we briefly present the main elements of our own considered public argument. Second, we share some activities, exercises, and questions that should encourage further reflection of the many issues raised so far. Third, we include a list of books and articles that are resources for further reading and discussion. In Part II we stated that many teachers identify with the points raised in all three public arguments. Most of us have views of teaching, learning, and schooling that are more diverse than "traditional," "typical," or "middle of the road" perspectives. Indeed, we recognize this fact as integral to who we are, what we do, what we think is best for others, and what we hope for. All people have an orientation, and ours mostly lies within the disability-centered perspective. By this we mean that one of our major concerns is the way in which people with disabilities have experienced a history of misunderstanding, marginalization, segregation, exclusion, and devaluation—both in and out of education systems (Solomon, 2013). We are motivated by ways in which we can continue to create and support educational settings in which *all* students are valued and provided with a rigorous curriculum in inclusive contexts.

There are reasons why we articulate our views here. After all, no text is without assumptions. However, at the same time we have endeavored to create a book that would not ground you in a single, particular direction, complete with (usually unstated) biases. We have, rather, created a text that requires you, your professor, and your peers to raise vitally important issues and reflect upon them. We recognize that it is also important for you to be aware of our own assumptions and biases because you should know where *all* authors stand (and question why authors of many traditional "jumbo" educational textbooks do not seem to take one). It is crucial, we believe, that we offer an example of a public argument that is perhaps less well known. Although the disability-centered view is, in fact, close to our own, at times we may bring in elements that are from other public arguments. We share our own way of synthesizing many elements that provide our grounding or disposition within education because it is essential that you, too, begin to articulate your own views and assumptions.

In the first volume of this series, *Reflective Teaching*, the authors emphasized the active and reflective roles of both the prospective and practicing teacher. A different way to think further about the topics raised in this book is to continue questioning, both formally and informally, the everyday common practices within our culture and society. We believe visiting traditional and special schools, talking with teachers, chatting with parents, interacting with children, analyzing texts, unpacking stereotypic and non-stereotypic representations, evaluating potential teaching resources, and so on, will help you continue growing as thoughtful, informed educators. We include some suggestions with the hope that you will try some, engage with the topics they raise and the questions they pose, and constantly further reflect upon implications for you as a teacher.

Finally, we provide a list of articles, books, videos, and webpages to which we have referred in this text—along with others that we have found useful in our career as teacher educators. The majority of these texts are available at your college or local library, and the articles can be accessed through library-sponsored search engines.

DISABILITY, TEACHING, AND SCHOOLS: AN ABBREVIATED VIEW

What to Do?

The issues raised by contemplating disability, teaching, and schooling are complex, resisting any simple, singular approach. Multiple questions come to mind, such as:

1   How do we create and sustain more equitable educational opportunities?

2   How do we ensure that all children are provided with equal resources in our society that historically has been, and currently is, essentially unequal?

3   How can we rethink and reframe disability to become dis/ability, namely, viewing every student primarily through a strength-based lens?

4   How can we better understand that when combined with race and class, disabled students are subjectified to marginalization within marginalization, discrimination within discrimination?

5   How can we combat multiple forms of discrimination that students experience?

We recognize that there are no quick and easy answers, no magic bullets, no panaceas to rectify this complex, ongoing, and to some readers—if we are honest—daunting situation. When we look at the record of public schooling, the picture is often paradoxical and disheartening (Cuban, 1993). On one hand, schooling is viewed as the great equalizer of all citizens. On the other hand, it has never automatically provided for all citizens, and the inclusion of groups such as females, poor children, immigrants, African Americans, second language learners, and children with disabilities have come after long struggles by those groups to gain access to education (Zinn, 2005). As Liston and Zeichner (1996) have pointed out:

> In fact we are not a society that devotes much of our substantial resources to our students or children. Our society is class-based, racially divided, and essentially masculinist in its orientation. Greed and consumerism are at its core. The accumulation of wealth and status are its motivating forces (p. 85).

Here we will add to the formidable challenges of racism, classism, and sexism the phenomenon of *ableism*. As with the other forceful forms of oppression that precede it, ableism is so pervasive that it seems to saturate almost every aspect of life—yet very few people name it as such and openly acknowledge it. We believe it worth pausing to take a deeper look into what ableism actually is, how it looks, and implications for educators. Rauscher and McClintock (1996) have described ableism as:

> A pervasive system of discrimination and exclusion that oppresses people who have mental, emotional, and physical disabilities. . . . Deeply rooted beliefs about health, productivity, beauty, and the value of human life, perpetuated by the public and private media, combine to create an

environment that is often hostile to those whose physical, mental, cognitive, and sensory abilities ... who fall out of the scope of what is currently defined as socially acceptable (p.198).

Here, the authors call attention to the status of humans who are devalued because they have been deemed to fall outside the circle of normalcy collectively drawn by many forces within society. Those lines are often shrugged off by those considered non-disabled as simply, "That's just the way it is." This commonplace response led journalist-activist Joseph Shapiro (1993) to flatly state, "Nondisabled Americans do not understand disabled ones" (p. 1).

Valle and Connor (2010) also point out non-recognition by able-bodied people of ableism, writing:

Forms of *ableism*—the belief that able-bodied people are superior to disabled people—range from subtle to blatant. In general, considered "less than" by their non-disabled counterparts, people with disabilities are ascribed second-class status, and experience a different sense of reality. A luxury of privilege is not having to think about one's status. Just as European-Americans rarely think about the benefits inherent in their skin color, able-bodied people are privileged in not having to think about things that disabled people *must* contemplate. For example, when planning a simple trip to a restaurant, an able-bodied person does not have to think about accessible public transportation, doorways, table-seating, and restrooms, because the world is configured with able-bodied people in mind (p. 18).

Here we see vastly different levels of consciousness pertaining to how people navigate through the same world very differently, a world that is either accessible or inaccessible, with little in-between. The forcefulness of ableism within schools and society paints a bleak picture that can render us immobile, feeling powerless in countering negativity toward disability on so many fronts. At the same time, we believe an integral part of life is to cultivate hope and recognize what *can be done* by individuals, groups, organizations, and societies—to change beliefs, practices, and norms with view to making life better for all groups within a democracy. Disabled scholar and activist Paul Longmore (2003), while acknowledging the profundity of disabled people's ongoing struggles in all aspects of society, also commented, "Perhaps the greatest progress toward the integration of people with disabilities has appeared in the U.S. public schools" (p. 26). So, we must take stock that some progress has been made—even though there is still a long, long way to go.

THE PERMANENCE OF ABLEISM AND NECESSARY ACTION

Over the course of our own professional experiences, as two career-long educators who began as teachers within segregated special education classes, we have come to see ableism as a force that undergirds all aspects of schooling. These include: student configurations in classrooms; inclusive classrooms; segregated classrooms; physical location of space; federal, state, and local policies; teacher education programs; curriculum; materials; teacher dispositions; administrative structures; financing; recreation; socialization; tracking; and so on. Due to the omnipresence of ableism in structures and the seeming permanence of ableism in people's thoughts, we believe that such social injustices toward students with disabilities can and must be addressed.

We reflect upon what does social justice actually mean for disabled students and the educators who work with them? Some readers may likely argue that the very structure of special education is a form of social justice. After all, hasn't the passage of major U.S. law P.L. 94–142 (*Education for All Handicapped Children Act*, 1975) and its subsequent reauthorizations as *Individuals with Disabilities Education Act* (1990, 1997) and *Individuals with Disabilities Education Improvement Act* (2004) guaranteed a free and appropriate public education for all students with disabilities since 1975? The majority of traditional scholars working within the field of special education would argue that the field of special education does constitute social justice (for example, Anastasiou & Kauffman, 2011). However, at the same time, the field has also been constantly critiqued *because of* the educational structures that America has constructed and used to educate students with disabilities (Skrtic, 1991). In fact, despite good intentions embedded within protective law, and progress achieved as noted by Longmore (2003), the experiences of and outcomes for students with disabilities call for change.

For example, in comparison to their able-bodied peers, disabled students in the special education system are likely to have: low graduation rates (Advocates for Children, 2005), a lengthier time completing school (U.S. Department of Education, 2005), high drop out rates (Thurlow, Sinclair, & Johnson, 2002), unemployment or underemployment (Moxley & Finch, 2003), less likelihood of entering college and more likelihood of leaving without graduating (Gregg, 2007), and higher rates of incarceration (Children's Defense Fund, 2007). In the special education system, students still experience segregation according to disability, with students of color and/or from linguistic minorities continuing to be placed in more restrictive settings based on some of the most stigmatizing labels (Gabel, Curcic,

Powell, Khader, & Albee, 2009; Losen & Orfield, 2002). As has been argued elsewhere (Ferri & Connor, 2005), when it became illegal to segregate schools by race, separation according to disability occurred as a loophole to permit ongoing racial divisions. For many scholars interested in education *and* disability, the very idea of "Special Education" is problematic because it represents a monopoly of thought about these two related concepts, and signifies a variety of meanings to different people—from a benevolent, enabling system of services and protections (Kauffman & Hallahan, 1995) to a disabling structure, oppressive in nature that functions as a precursor to unemployment, low-paying jobs, and jail (Karagiannis, 2000; Kim, Losen, & Hewitt, 2010). Unsurprisingly, these troubling outcomes follow the same patterns around the world, as has been seen in recent research from Argentina, Austria, Germany, India, Kenya, South Africa, Sweden, the UK, and the US (Artiles, Kozleski, & Waitoller, 2011).

Divisions within the field of special education have existed since its inception (see, for example, Danforth, 2009; Dunn, 1968; Wang, Reynolds, & Walberg, 1986), but the field has been highly unreceptive—even hostile—to critiques. Influential figures have frequently silenced potentially productive discussions, limiting a variety of perspectives, and asserting an ideological "orthodoxy" beyond questioning (Gallagher, Heshusius, Iano, & Skrtic, 2004). At the turn of the twenty-first century, a gathering of renowned special education scholars met to debate "the divide" in their field between subgroups of traditionalists and reconceptualists. These two "sides" illustrated the depth of this split: the former, advocating to stay the course, the latter desirous to re-imagine and redevelop how disabled students are educated (Andrews et al., 2000).

For many years, people with disabilities have critiqued the dispositions, conceptualizations, and motivations of disability-focused researchers, reminding them of how their work minimally impacts upon the material lives of people with disabilities. Oliver (1996) has described most disability-related research as, ". . . at best irrelevant, and at worst, oppressive" (p. 129). In contrast, scholars of disability who are disabled themselves often make explicit links to their lives and professions with issues of social justice, access, and activism (Asch, 2001; Fine & Asch, 2003; Gabel & Peters, 2004; Linton, 2006; Wendell, 2000).

Reframing Disability as Human Diversity

We are interested in cultivating, understanding, differentiating among, and critiquing, many models of disability. As discussed earlier in this text, the most prevalent conceptualization of disability is the medical model. However, much ground has been gained by countering this with the social or sociocultural model of disability. (For a variety of other models of disability such as economic, religious, cultural, expert, moral, market, spectrum, etc. see www.disabled-world.com/definitions/disability-models.php)

The Medical Model. The major critique of special education has been its dogged adherence to conceptualizations of disability primarily grounded in science, medicine, and psychology, all of which frame disability as dysfunction, deficit, and disorder that is intrinsic to the student (Dudley-Marling & Gurn, 2011). The language of special education is full of medical terminology that imbues its practices with the authority of pseudo-science. For example, Valle and Connor (2010) describe assessment, eligibility, and special placement procedures delineated under Individuals with Disabilities Education Improvement Act of 2004 as follows:

> The "patient" (student) presents with "symptoms" (educational problems). The "scientific expert" (school psychologist) performs an "examination" (psycho-educational assessment) in order to confirm or rule out a "diagnosis" (disability). Once a "diagnosis" (disability) is identified, a "prescription" (Individualized Education Plan, or IEP) is written with recommendations for a "course of treatment" (special education placement and individual instruction) intended to "cure" (remediate) the "patient" (student). A "follow-up appointment," (annual IEP review) is scheduled to evaluate the effectiveness of the "treatment plan" (special education services) (p. 40–41).

By pathologizing human difference as disability, the field of special education (and its foundational knowledge) has historically put forth a very narrow lens for teachers to understand students who have been classified as disabled.

The Social Model. Many educators, including critical special educators, find the field of special education to be inadequate in terms of how disability is conceptualized, and subsequently found more meaningful understandings within the interdisciplinary field of disability studies. Instead of being grounded in scientific, medical, psychological, and legal frameworks, disability studies is rooted in a more sociological or "social model" understanding of disability as a phenomenon primarily created by social, cultural, and historical forces (Linton, 1998).

Assigned positions outside of social norms, people with disabilities have asked: Who are positioned on the inside of the norm, and who on the outside? Who becomes advantaged and, conversely, who becomes disadvantaged by this arrangement? Who (re)creates that norm? Why has it been reproduced? Where? When? Where do we stand (or sit, or lie) in relation to that norm? Such questions allow us to see the ways in which society is profoundly normalized. Indeed, the process and achievement of normalcy can be seen, in part, as enormous pressure from many sources. As Davis (2002) notes,

> Whether we are talking about AIDS, low birth weight babies, special education issues, euthanasia, and the thousand other topics listed in the newspapers every day, the examination, discussion, anatomizing this form of "difference" is nothing less than a desperate attempt by people to consolidate their normalcy (p. 117).

Given this much-needed focus on interrogating the concept of normalcy, rather than creating it (as the institution of special education does), the sociocultural model of disability has very different priorities than a medical model perspective.

Juxtaposing Two Major Dispositions. Although elements of both models have been woven throughout this text, we believe juxtaposing them in a concentrated manner will help the reader to see their direct connection to difficult questions that we've raised pertaining to the "rule of normalcy" within schools, and the role of special education in fortifying the oppressive and ultimately artificial binaries of normal-abnormal. This comparison helps us understand, with view to questioning how inflexible school practices such as standardized norms, ability tracking, age and grade level "appropriate" expectations, ritualized behaviors, and heavily bureaucratized practices of documentation of disability, all function as interlocking cogs vital in perpetuating the machinery of normalcy, making Baker (2002) conclude that everyday practices are actively mobilized toward "the hunt for disability" (p. 663). Furthermore, the high numbers of students labeled disabled is evidence of an educational obsession to locate, and then often *relocate*, children who are not deemed as sufficiently approximating normalcy in terms of how bodies are expected to function within classrooms (exhibiting certain desired ways of learning, focusing, following instructions, behaving, speaking correctly, and so on).

In the following section, we show the two models provide a very different disposition toward perceiving, and therefore responding to, human differences.

1. Conceptualizations of Disability

A Medicalized Lens. The primary understanding is that disability is a deficit that exists within an individual, and is therefore something to ". . . cure, accommodate, or endure" (Andrews et al., 2000, p. 258).

- It is fixed, permanent, "owned" by the person, and is the person's "responsibility."

A Sociocultural Lens. Disability is constituted by the *interaction* between student characteristics and the context of the environment.

- It is relative to the dynamics enacted among all humans.

2. The Purpose of Schools

A Medicalized Lens. Schooling is predicated upon the mastery of skills and strategies such as in reading, writing, and mathematics across content areas.

- Literacy is perceived as deciphering a text.

A Sociocultural Lens. Schooling is about increased awareness (and acquisition) of ways in which we and others think, act, talk in different situations, and the power of knowing how to do this. For example: differences in talking and behaving within a specific group (siblings, friends, classmates, professors); thinking and strategizing within diverse social situations; knowing about knowing; how to do school and academics "right" and why; and so on.

- Literacy is about deciphering, and participation in, social practices.

3. The Nature of Learning

A Medicalized Lens. Learning is an individual process, typically achieved one-to-one, or via small group instruction.

- The learner only acquires knowledge from the teacher.

- Learning is atomistic, with an emphasis placed on discrete parts.
- Learning is classroom specific.
- Learners work with others of a similar level.
- Learning is assumed to be additive.

A Sociocultural Lens. Learning is an inherently social interactive process. By working with others, students become socialized into strategies and practices that help them learn knowledge and skills. Learning is internalized mostly through dialogic interactions.

- Knowledge is acquired through a reciprocal relationship between teacher and learner. Each has agency, and the ability to transform the discourse.
- Learning is holistic, with an emphasis placed on discrete parts.
- Learning is grounded in history and culture (i.e. people achieve more sophisticated ways of thinking through the use of social and cultural tools that have historic significance).
- Learners work in heterogeneous groups so that they can "grow into" the behavior.
- The assumption is that learning is recursive, non-linear.

4. The Role of the Teacher

A Medicalized Lens. Grounded in positivist research with "scientific" claims, instruction is teacher directed.

- Skills are taught in isolation, frequently in rote style.
- Teaching leads to development via reinforcement.

A Sociocultural Lens. Grounded in constructivist research, instruction is student-centered.

- Authentic learning occurs within a specific context.
- Teaching leads the development of students. The teacher and students constantly interact, always negotiating towards the student's zone of proximal development (Vygotsky, 1987).

5. Instruction

A Medicalized Lens. Instruction is conceived of as explanation and practice.

- Instruction is usually a highly plotted lesson, oftentimes commercially packaged and known as "teacher-proof."
- Mistakes and errors are avoided.

A Sociocultural Lens. Instruction is conceived of as interpersonal and fluid, guided by the teacher whose goal is the gradual release of responsibility. A building of knowledge and/or acquisition of skills occur through the acquisition of the discourse.

- Instruction is contingent on several factors; teachers constantly observe, evaluate, and then redirect or extend student behaviors (i.e. scaffold or mediate their performance).
- Errors and mistakes are considered insightful keys to understanding students. The teacher observes students as an integral part of working within the zone of proximal development.

6. Failure

A Medicalized Lens. Failure is the inability to adequately perform strategies and skills expected in schools.

- Failure is located within the child.

A Sociocultural Lens. Failure is predicated upon the overall quality of schooling, including adequate resources and access to school-based discourses.

- A learning environment created by the teacher determines the degree of student success or failure.

By sharply juxtaposing these two broad belief systems that influence teacher dispositions, we have begun to reveal ways in which they can strategize to plan and teach all students. In the following sections we look at some other approaches we believe are helpful.

OUR EDUCATIONAL STRATEGIES

By reframing disability as a phenomenon to view through different and/or multiple lenses allows educators, scholars, people deemed disabled and able-bodied, to contemplate disability in more rich and nuanced ways, serving to expand our collective understanding of bodily differences. The very notion of "disability" becomes interrogated as a marker of identity that we take for granted, offering us new ways of looking at familiar things.

The preceding section demonstrates how important it is that each educator ask themselves: "Through what lens do I view disability?" Our own preference for primarily viewing disability through a sociocultural perspective (while culling from others, as needed) reveals our disposition toward human differences that have been *signified* through the beliefs and practices of our culture as disabilities. As you have seen, the belief systems of teachers influence their general disposition within education and that, in turn, informs all of the numerous decisions they must make on a daily basis pertaining to: conceptualizations of disability; the purpose of schools; the nature of learning; the role of a teacher; the purpose and type of instruction; and what constitutes student failure and success.

Our own driving educational strategy has been to challenge the unquestioned orthodoxy of special education within the field of education. As critical special educators who write within both special education and the field of disability studies, we seek to engage knowledge claims about disability in all arenas including research, college seminars, teacher lounges, K-12 classes, and with friends and family around dinner tables. As Gallagher (2004) has pointed out, "This conversation is of crucial importance because it confronts the fundamental frameworks within which the debates over full inclusion, disability definitions, labeling, and the like are deliberated" (p. vii). At the heart of this debate is our belief, along with Goffman (1963), that "The normal and the stigmatized are not persons but rather perspectives" (p. 137).

So, you might ask, what are some effective ways and educational strategies that we have utilized in our careers as teachers and teacher educators? In this section we highlight several key ways that we hope will serve as a beginning for new teachers entering into, and seasoned teachers within, the profession of education. These include: always being aware of our assumptions of disability and being open to change; actively challenging ableism; building inclusive classroom communities; employing flexible approaches to planning curricula, units, lessons, and activities; keeping a critical eye on elements within current reform movements.

We believe that, as educators, we must maintain a constant awareness of our assumptions about disability, and be open to change. Variation among humans is virtually infinite, and there's no one who is able to know everything about one particular disability label, let alone all of them. What we do urge, however, is for all educators to reflect on their sources of knowledge and understanding. How have these sources come to form and build understanding disability for that person? If sources are from text-books, the *Diagnostic and Statistical Manual-IV* (1994), research articles, "conservative"-based webpages, and professors who support this inform-ation, then the person only knows disability from a deficit-based view. In contrast, if sources are from narratives and life stories of people with disabilities, interviews, documentaries, research articles with a disability studies framework, direct knowledge of a family member, and so on, then the person comes to know disability from a much more complicated socially-aware view. We realize the risk of oversimplification here, know-ing that information about disability is not always so clearly delineated into two camps of thought, medical and sociocultural, but often overlaps within each person's knowledge.

That said, we believe that the former scenario is likely to subconsciously reinforce ableism, and the latter scenario is likely to challenge it. One of our ways to strategize working within education has been to actively chal-lenge ableism. Given we have established its omnipresence, challenging ableism can occur at so many levels, including the individual, interac-tional, institutional, societal, and historical. For example, at the personal level we can analyze any representation of disability that we see (in print, online, on TV, in film, in textbooks, etc.) and, if it stereotypes, limits, or devalues people, we can respond to it. In our conversations with people, when put downs occur within language, such as "That's retarded," or "You're such a spaz," we can point out how language is used to demean people with disabilities. At the institutional level, when we engage with peers and colleagues who have not had the opportunity to encounter different ways of framing or understanding disability, we can use the moment to introduce alternative ideas and perspectives that are more disability-centered. This can be very important in leveraging change toward more inclusive practices, as the civil rights of children and the preferences of their families are not always considered before teacher opinions (remember Jesse in Case Study 2?). In addition, we must always ask: *What* is being taught about disabilities? Chances are, it's usually very little—if anything—and what is taught is likely to be framed in either a deficit and/or charitable discourse. Teachers can make sure that disability-centered teaching about disability is an integral part of the curriculum. At the societal level, we can be aware of accessibility in all public services venues and support efforts to increase access to basic things such as transportation and community spaces. At the historical level we can contribute to conversations, projects, and curricula by incorporating and reclaiming the voices of people with disabilities who have not been represented (Fleischer & Zames, 2001).

Of course the main strategy for which we advocate is the building of inclusive classroom communities, places in which all students "fit" and feel welcome. We realize that this can be a lot of work, but feel it worthwhile as it is an educator's responsibility to do their very best in making sure that all students feel safe, respected, and supported in their academic, social, and emotional growth. Teachers can do this by getting to know their students well through a variety of interactions and activities. In addition, teachers can talk with students' parents, previous teachers, as well as work very closely with all support staff such as paraprofessionals and teacher's aides.

The biggest help, we believe, to the actual nitty-gritty of everyday teaching is for teachers to become acquainted with, and comfortable using, Universal Design for Learning (UDL) and differentiated instruction. UDL is based on the simple premise of universal design within architecture, that is, if architects build the edifice/space with everyone in mind from the start, then that allows everyone access—and they can be included without the need to retrofit original plans. This premise, transferred to the classroom, means teachers are educational architects who should create their curriculum, units, lessons, activities, and assessments with all students in mind from the beginning—thereby lessening or eliminating the need to significantly modify plans when moving forward (Burghstaler, 1999).

On her book cover *Because We Can Change the World* (2000/2010), Mara Sapon-Shevin's subtitle states "a practical guide to building cooperative, inclusive classroom communities." Sapon-Shevin's work is thankfully one of several good UDL-inspired resources to assist teachers in creating supportive classroom communities through addressing social issues. Her guidance is sage, as she acknowledges the need to have a strong vision in order to create change, and identify and work against challenges to that vision. However, optimism must triumph, as all educators need hope in going forward with their work, and having a sense that they are contributing in positive ways to change the world. The areas that Sapon-Shevin urges us to focus on include: the ability to share ourselves with others; coming to know others well; creating a place where everybody belongs; setting goals and giving and getting support; working collaboratively to learn; speaking the truth; and acting powerfully.

Another practical volume that supports our vision is *Joyful Learning: Active and Collaborative Learning in Inclusive Classrooms* by Alice Udvari-Solner and Paula Kluth (2008). Here, the authors have compiled successful teaching strategies that promote interactions leading to learning among all students, for a variety of purposes such as building teams, engaging students in the process of learning, studying, and reviewing, creating active lectures, and assessing students. A shorter practitioner-based text that is disability-centered is Valle and Connor's (2010) *Rethinking Disability: A Disability Studies Approach to Inclusive Practices*, complete with suggestions to challenge the omnipresence of ableism in schools and society. Other more traditional texts include works by Friend and Bursuck (2011) and Salend (2010). While they feature many worthwhile recommended teaching practices, and highlight the benefits of collaborating with co-teachers and other support professionals, they are also fairly "safe" in not deviating too far from traditional special education texts.

The increased focus on differentiated instruction as an answer to working with students who have diverse needs within a single classroom encompasses disabled students. In particular, the work of Carol Ann Tomlinson (1999; 2001) has influenced how teachers approach planning, as she encourages them to see the value and effectives of being flexible in many domains within teaching. These domains include the *content* (what is being taught), the *process* (how it is being taught, how students are engaged in learning), and the *product* (the evidence students produce as a result of the teacher's teaching and their own learning). Each one of these domains merits in-depth study, along with how all three are integral phases of a lesson. In addition, Tomlinson suggests that teachers also incorporate student readiness levels, interests, and learning profiles (what they're good at, and what they need strengthening). These approaches to teaching are compatible with UDL, and can at first seem quite intricate and layered. However, with practice, and confidence-building, teachers are able to create learning environments and lessons that can reach all students at their current level—and support them in their efforts to get to the next stage in their individual growth.

In addition to the constant acquisition of practical knowledge, we also hope that teachers continue to read worthwhile disability-centered sources that challenge deeply entrenched assumptions by advocating multiple ways to understand human differences. One such text is Andrew Solomon's (2013) *Far From the Tree,* a book centered on parents, their unexpected children "outside of the norm," and ways parents found to make their families "work." As a dyslexic gay father, Solomon's personal experience propelled him to explore ways in which children defying the familial adage of "the apple doesn't fall far from the tree" force family members to expand their thinking about *all things* including love, belonging, and both individual and collective identity. After asserting that "Ability is a tyranny of the majority" (p. 29), he counters this state of affairs by narrating the lives of people battling this form of oppression, who ". . . at the most basic level . . . [seek to] find accommodation of difference rather than erasure of it" (p. 27). In many ways, we see close parallels between initial parental responses and how teachers feel when a disabled child unexpectedly enters their classroom for the first time, perhaps triggering fear, panic, anxiety, feelings of inadequacy, and even misfortune ("Why me?"). We acknowledge that it is not without irony when teachers have much to learn about children from families. However, after all, families are the site of where acceptance of diversity and inclusion into a network of relationships evolves naturally. When Solomon explains "This book's conundrum is that most of the families described here have ended up grateful for experiences they would have done anything to avoid" (p. 47), his sentiment can be echoed by many teachers who have learned more through engaging with disabled children than they could have ever imagined.

On another note, we also believe that teachers should keep a critical eye on elements within current reform movements and always ask themselves: *What's best for kids?* While few, if any, would argue against having high standards, for example, we must still value children who may never reach them or "fit the mold" constructed by the standards. Let us be clear. We want every child to reach his or her maximum potential in terms of academics. However, we care deeply for students who cannot reach these standards, and many are those categorized as having disabilities. Such policies may raise scores of a minority of disabled students, but the majority is further disabled through their "failure" to obtain an academic high school diploma that leads to more barriers in terms of employment and further education. The "double-speak" of major reforms can be seen in two of its policies *No Child Left Behind* and *Race For the Top*. If we race for the top for competitive funds then the winners triumph over the losers, who have, in essence, been left behind.

In closing, to reiterate, we advocate for the centering of disability in education—from K-12 classes and beyond, to teacher education programs that continue to sort and separate potential teachers into general and special educators. As disability-activist Marta Russell (1998) has asserted on the cover of her book, disability is "at the end of the social contract." We must counter this situation by providing different ways to understand disability, teaching children with disabilities more effectively and inclusively, working against ableism.

EXERCISES FOR FURTHER REFLECTION

So far, we have used either case studies or written public arguments as the basis of our reflections. We designed the case studies and public arguments in the hope of encouraging you to think about connections between classroom actions, educational policy, and your own experiences and beliefs. In this final section, we thought it would be helpful to suggest further possible experiences, most of which go beyond a written text, that would likely create further reflection on disability and teaching. In the suggestions that follow we have endeavored to create additional opportunities that may provide engagement with actual people, schools, and organizations about the substantial issues that have been raised throughout this text.

Recommendations

Before listing some potential experiences, we wanted to take a moment and bring a few things to your attention. Regardless of whether you are new to the profession, or a seasoned educator, we all tend to "jump in" to situations we observe in schools and classrooms with our judgment of what's going on and why. It can be very tricky to view classroom interactions or school policies that appear to impact a student's experiences and not to interpret the scene or setting. However, it is precisely that interpretation that we want to hold up as the focus of your reflections. We hope you will note your reactions to things said and things seen.

We believe part of good teaching is having a critical reflective awareness about how our interpretations of what we see or hear influences how we teach to enable or disable, provide access or erect barriers, nurture or diminish students. As we have seen in Case Study 2 when Shelly, the special educator, and Judith, the general educator, interpret Jesse's appearance, abilities, and work produced quite differently.

When you read each possible suggestion, and choose the ones that interest you the most, be mindful of separating what is observed from your reactions. Liston and Zeichner (1996) have shared:

> It is helpful, in fact it is necessary, to learn how to disentangle our interpretations from the scenes we observe and the experiences we have. In our own

work observing student teachers we have found it very helpful to try to jot down notes, descriptions of actual interactions, and when we have noticeable personal reactions or interpretations to note those separately. What is key here is that we try to be aware of our judgment and reactions, attempt to separate those interpretations from the events and experiences . . . we want to suggest that when you engage in the experiences or observations outlined here, it will be important that you recognize and listen to your reactions, disentangle those reactions from your description of "events," and then reflect on both your reactions and the events (p. 93).

This way, we agree, your responses will be more nuanced and layered, providing you with ample areas to reflect upon as you negotiate the complexities of education in the lives of people.

Importantly, observations and experiences are more authentic if you are already part of a school, as a teacher, student teacher, or experiencing a fieldwork assignment consistently at one site. For experiences outside of schools in institutions, organizations, or with individuals, we ask that you consider offering some of your time or help. We share this so you don't go forward in these suggested assignments as a "taker" of information, but also a contributor or provider of sorts. Do resist rushing, speeding up, or "checking off" such assignments. Instead, take your time to know the experiences and realities of other people in settings that you are not familiar with. We know from our own college course assignments taken over several decades ago that such insightful visits and revealing interviews have the power to stay within us and influence us throughout our education careers.

RECOMMENDATIONS

Visit a Totally Segregated School. Most school districts still have schools or programs in which some disabled students are placed for the majority, if not all, of their education. Sometimes, these are public institutions, and at other times, they are private institutions in which students are educated at public expense. Meet and talk with the director of the school about its purpose and mission. Chat with the teachers and support personnel about their perspectives on what disabled children can learn. We realize that, just like differences among non-disabled children, learning abilities and inabilities vary enormously. Oftentimes, such specialized environments are provided for students who have "low incidence" disabilities such as blindness, deafness, deaf-blindness, autism, and Down Syndrome. At other times, students with more common labels such as having a "cognitive impairment" or "emotional disturbance" can also be placed in the settings. Observe some classes and note the content and skills being taught, methods teachers are using, and opportunities that students have to engage in learning. Contemplate what are the benefits and/or drawbacks of such a setting?

Visit a Segregated Special Education Classroom. The majority of schools, regardless of urban, suburban, or rural settings, still have a sizeable number of segregated special education classrooms in which disabled students spend all or part of their day. Talk with the teacher about his or her students. How are they viewed? How are their disabilities understood in terms of the medical or social model of understanding disability? Observe a lesson and analyze the type and frequency of interactions between the teacher and students, as well as opportunities for student-to-student thoughts, ideas, and work-in-progress. How is teaching students individualized? Ask the teacher to describe his or her understandings about the role and responsibilities of a special educator to students and general educators. Contemplate what are the benefits and/or drawbacks of such a setting?

Visit an Inclusive Classroom. Most schools now have inclusive classrooms, although they vary enormously in terms of quality and effectiveness. Unfortunately, many such classrooms do not differ from general education classrooms in which instruction is delivered without much, if any, differentiation according to student needs. On the other hand, there are some excellent models that reveal ways in which teachers have worked together and collaborated to ensure that all students would have access to all aspects of the curriculum including quizzes, exams, group work, materials, and so on. Observe a class being taught and watch how all students are integrated into the lesson by the questions asked, tasks expected, and evidence of work that they share. How were materials used? How were questions varied? In what ways were children treated differently and the same? If there was more than one teacher, or there was a teacher's aide or paraprofessional in the room, in what ways did they work together to support students? How do the teachers in this school define "inclusion" and how do their definitions compare to the ones you are discussing in class?

Read Some of the Research Literature on Collaborative Teaching. Working with another teacher can be extremely rewarding, especially within a teacher's first few years of teaching. There's nothing like an expert showing you the ropes! Until recently, the history of teaching has meant educators were working in what Thomas Hehir (2011) has described as "egg crates," meaning they were all next to each other, but working in isolation. However, the inclusion movement has inspired team teaching to become a reality. Oftentimes, the combination consists of a general and a special educator who work together with a view to supporting all students. How this is done is different among departments, schools, districts, and regions. Nonetheless, a growing body of teacher-friendly research has grown in this area, complete with advice and tips from former classroom teachers and researchers. See, for example, the work of Gately and Gately (2001) who call attention to different domains within the collaborative classroom, ranging from how to maximize the use of instructional planning tome to physical space, from classroom management to student assessment. In addition, Murawski's and Dieker's work (2008) focuses on the importance of building and maintaining professional relationships for the benefit of all students.

Observe a Child with a Visible Disability in a Classroom. Some educators and administrators have been heard to say, "It was a great inclusive classroom—because you couldn't tell which students were special ed." While well intentioned, this type of comment is patronizing, and misses the point that disability *should* be visible in many, if not most, classrooms. The pains taken to keep it from being noticeable can actually reinforce ableist attitudes about superiority, and create further stigmatism of students with disabilities. We are not saying shout it from the rooftops that certain students are disabled, but José's cerebral palsy will be noticeable if he publicly responds to a teacher's question, Keisha's worksheet may have different problems because of her cognitive impairment, and Brian may be orally explaining his answer to a teacher in some part of the room because of his dysgraphia (a pervasive struggle to write). What are the instances in which educators provide access to the curriculum for the student? In what instances is the student denied access through physical, attitudinal, or pedagogical barriers? Be extremely careful not to single out the child during an observation. One suggestion is to always observe the child along with non-disabled students.

Observe a Child with an Invisible Disability in a Classroom. The notion of visible vs. invisible disabilities can be controversial, even within the academic field of disability studies. After all, having an invisible disability can, depending on how it's looked at, claim an "upside" (having the power to choose whether or not to disclose one's disability status; so-called "passing") and a "downside" (conversely, not feeling represented or acknowledged). Also, often seen as "mild" or "high incidence" disabilities, what we have come to know as learning disabilities, speech and language disorders, emotional disturbance, and cognitive impairment make up for approximately 85% of all children with disabilities (Hehir, Figueroa, Gamm, Katzman, Gruner, Karger, & Hernandez, 2005). In brief, the majority of students have invisible disabilities. When observing a child identified as having an invisible disability, how does he or she respond to the teacher's instruction, questioning, task assigned, assessments? In what ways does the teacher provide support? Does invisibility mean that these students "fall through the cracks"? In what ways do students attempt to conform to normalcy at all cost? In what ways do students not "fit the mold," even though they ostensibly look like they do? Be extremely careful not to single out the child during an observation. One suggestion is to always observe the child along with non-disabled students.

Interview a Parent of a Disabled Child.   Talk with a parent about their experiences of having a disabled child. What was their initial response? How did they react? How receptive was the school to their child? To what degree do they believe it is necessary to advocate for their child? To what degree has the disability impacted the child's life in and out of school? How has it impacted the family's life? What life lessons have been learned by the parent? Listening to parents of disabled children can provide incredible insights into so many things: disability as difference; school systems; classroom interactions; friendships; ableism; reframing negative associations with disability into positive ones. Research with parents have revealed them to be the primary source of belief in their children, even when school systems try to reject their input (Valle, 2009). Furthermore, their "expertise" can be more valuable than all of the research articles read because they have known their children in ways and across time that educational institutions are unable to do so. In particular, ask in what ways they understand their child differs from the school's understanding? How do they believe they can best help teachers know their child?

Interview an Adult with a Disability.   Talk to an adult who has a disability to find out ways in which that disability impacted schooling. The conversation may raise practical issues around memorable classroom experiences, student friendships, supportive teachers, rising to challenges posed by the curriculum—in short, everything that a non-disabled child experiences. At the same time, the conversation may yield sensitive issues around stigmatization, bullying, unsupportive teachers, and struggles with schoolwork. The person can comment upon changes witnessed since he or she attended school, in addition to experiences with college, the work place, and support systems (formal and informal). We realize the "taboo" element of directly talking about disability for many people, but believe the experiences and thoughts of people with disabilities can have a profoundly positive impact on educators in their knowledge of working with children.

Interview a Disability-Activist.   Progress toward the inclusion of children with disabilities in schools and society over the past half-century could not have been achieved without disability rights advocates. People with disabilities, their parents, and their allies have played a crucial role in mobilizing to forge laws, demonstrate about injustices, enlighten, provide testimonies, protest inequities, and educate. Discuss ways in which the person has contributed to the general fight for access and equity. At what age did the person become aware of inequities? Why did the person become politicized? What actions were taken as an individual and/or as part of a group? What does a person think about how schools respond to disability? What were some of the person's school experiences and how did that influence their life? What are some changes in society that the person would like to see?

Analyze Curriculum Resources.   Read a sample of the district's mission statement. Where and how are students with disabilities featured? Then read a school's curriculum with an eye to both (1) looking for how disability is represented, and (2) how the curriculum can potentially be adapted in ways that support UDL. Regarding representations of disability: Are they present or absent? If they're present, to what degree do the representations reinforce or challenge stereotypes? If they reinforce, what are some ways to counter such representations? Regarding curriculum: What are some ways in which teachers can engage all students within any given lesson? How might types and levels of questioning vary? How might tasks designed to engage students in specific content knowledge be differentiated? How might evidence of student knowledge vary, depending upon who is within the class?

Analyze Representations in the Media.   The media is notorious for portraying people with disabilities in very limited ways that include being: a villain, a monster, a revenger, bitter at society, an object of pity, infantilized, having special powers, suicidal, and inspirational (for further reading on this subject, see Safran, 1998a, 1998b). In many ways, disability can be seen as "everywhere and nowhere." It is everywhere as it is somehow featured in every film, and if it is not, its absence is present. Commonplace depictions are nowhere in terms of how accurately it portrays the everyday lives of millions of people with disabilities. Re-watch your favorite movie or an episode of your favorite TV series and see which one of the above categories best fit the depiction of disability. What are the implications of such portrayals? How do they impact and shape children's perceptions of disability and difference? How do some documentaries attempt to redress the balance of inaccurate portrayals of disability? How can films be used to actively teach about disability (Connor & Bejoian, 2006)?

Explore Web Pages.   Given the ubiquitous nature of the Internet as a primary source of information, it is interesting to explore a variety of websites to find resources and evaluate the information shared, and determine which categories of the three broad categories used in this book most closely approximate the site. "Disability-centered" websites include those that are primarily created by and for people with disabilities. Interesting examples we recently looked at include sites that focus on Aspergers Syndrome, Learning Disabilities, and Attention Deficit Hyperactivity Disorder (ADHD) (see lists at end of this chapter). "Liberal-progressive" websites feature disability as a form of natural diversity. "Conservative" websites are often charity or research-based but adhere to deficit models of understanding disabilities. In addition, there are educa-tional websites that are highly informational and practical for teachers, yet are still rooted in deficit-perspectives (see for instance, www.ldonline.com dedicated to learning disabilities). Compare and contrast one from each category of "conservative," "liberal-progressive," and "disability-centered." In what ways might these websites help educators understand disability? In what ways might they be reinforcing misunderstandings of disability?

Watch a Documentary About Inclusive Education.   There have been several influential documentary films made to look at the complex issue raised by inclusive education. One of the most recent is *Including Samuel* (Habib, 2008) in which the director and producer chronicles the birth and growth of his son, Samuel, who has cerebral palsy and a host of permanent medical concerns. In addition to Samuel, the director features half a dozen children and adults with a variety of disabilities, both within schools and society. The director's second film *Who Cares About Kelsey?* (Habib, 2012) focuses on students who are labeled behavior disordered, and the challenges they—and their teachers—face in schools. These informative films about including children with disabilities in school were preceded by other ground-breaking works such as *Educating Peter* (Goodwin & Wurzburg, 1992), *Graduating Peter* (Wurzburg, 2001), and *Going to School/Ir a La Escuela* (Cohen, 2001). Any of these are worth viewing to analyze how students are portrayed, how teachers are receptive, how schools respond to challenges of inclusion—as there is no "blue print," but lots of active problem solving as disabled students move forward in general education settings.

Survey Schools in Your District. If possible, visit a cross-section of schools in your district that educate students from different social classes to see how students with disabilities are placed and taught within different schools. Observe the general upkeep of the building, the amount of space provided in classrooms, the level of teacher enthusiasm. Compare the classroom environments for students categorized as general and special education in terms of level of work, student engagement, visible diversity of race, ethnicity, gender, and disability. Contrast schools in terms of physical upkeep, including size and location of classrooms, school libraries, gyms, and other facilities. How accessible are the buildings for students who use wheelchairs? What are the differences between schools in regard to general resources, quality of teaching, composition of classes, how students with disabilities are educated?

CONCLUSION

We realize that this is just the beginning and there are many other ways in which you can explore the topic of disability and schools. This short text will hopefully serve to heighten your awareness, and to provide you with tools, to be self-reflective practitioners—always ready to question "why?" of yourself and others in order to hone your craft. We believe that keeping all of your students front and center in your mind, their daily successes and struggles, will help you become a teacher who is responsive to their needs.

We wish you the best in your teaching career.

—S. G. & D. C.

APPENDIX A: PERSONAL NARRATIVES

The following list is a selection of first-person narratives about living life as a disabled person. These are excellent sources for teachers to understand the experiences and perspectives of disabled people.

Brown, C. (1955). *My left foot*. New York: Simon.

Brueggemann, B. J. (1999). *Lend me your ear: Rhetorical constructions of deafness*. Washington, DC: Gallaudet University Press.

Callahan, J. (1990). *Don't worry, he won't get far on foot*. New York: Vintage Books.

Claire, E. (1999). *Exile and pride*. Cambridge, MA: Southend Press.

Fadiman, A. (1997). *The spirit catches you and you fall down: A Hmong child, her American doctors, and the collision of two cultures*. New York: Farrar, Straus & Giroux.

Finger, A. (1998). *Past due: A story of disability, pregnancy and birth*. New York: Seal Press.

Finger, A. (2006). *Elegy for a disease: A personal and cultural history of polio*. New York: St. Martin's Press.

Fries, K. (1997). *Body remember*. New York: Penguin.

Fries, K. (Ed.) (1997). *Staring back: The disability experience from the inside out*. New York: Plume.

Grandin, T. (1995). *Thinking in pictures and other reports from my life with autism*. New York: Vintage Books.

Grealy, L. (1995). *Autobiography of a face*. New York: Harper.

Groce, E. (1990). *Everyone here speaks sign language*. Cambridge, MA: Harvard University Press.

Hall, K. (1988). *Asperger Syndrome, the universe, and everything*. London: Jessica Kingsley Publishers.

Hammerschmidt, E. (2004). *Born on the wrong planet*. West Long Beach, CA: Tyborne Hill Publishers.

Handler, L. (1999). *Twitch and shout: A Touretter's tale*. New York: Plume.

Hockenberry, J. (1995). *Moving violations: War zones, wheelchairs and declarations of independence*. New York: Hyperion.

Jacobson, D. S. (1999). *The question of David: A disabled mother's journey through adoption, family, and life*. North Charleston, SC: Create Space Independent Publishing Platform.

Kleege, G. (1999). *Sight unseen*. New Haven, CT: Yale University Press.

Klein, B. S. (1998). *Slow dance: A story of stroke, love and disability*. Berkeley, CA: Page Mill Press.

Knighton, R. (2007). *Cockeyed: An unsentimental take on blindness*. New York: Public Affairs.

Knipfel, J. (1999). *Slackjaw: A memoir*. New York: Berkley Books.

Krieger, S. (2005). *Things no longer there: A memoir of losing sight and finding vision*. Madison, WI: University of Wisconsin Press.

Kuusisto, S. (1998). *Planet of the blind: A memoir*. New York: The Dial Press.

Kuusisto, S. (2006). *Eavesdropping: A memoir of blindness and listening*. New York: Norton.

Lee, C., & Jackson, R. (1992). *Faking it: A look into the mind of a creative learner*. Portsmouth, NH: Boynton/Cook-Heinemann.

Linton, S. (2006). *My body politic*. Ann Arbor, MI: University of Michigan Press.

Little, J. (1996). *If it weren't for the honor I'd rather have walked: Previously untold tales of the journey to the ADA*. Cambridge, MA: Brookline Books.

Lorde, A. (1980). *The cancer journals*. San Francisco, CA: Aunt Lute Books.

Mairs, N. (1996). *Waist-high in the world: A life among the nondisabled*. Boston, MA: Beacon Press.

Mooney, J. (2007). *The short bus: A journey beyond normal*. New York: Henry Holt.

Mooney, J., & Cole, D. (2000). *Learning outside the lines: Two ivy league students with learning disabilities and ADHD give you the tools for academic success and educational revolution*. New York: Fireside.

Mukhopadhyay, T. R. (2003). *The mind tree: A miraculous child breaks the silence of autism*. New York: Arcade.

Osborn, C. (1998). *Over my head: A doctor's account of head injury from the inside looking out*. Kansas City, MO: Peripatetic Publishing.

Padden, C., & Humphries, T. (1988). *Deaf in America: Voices from a culture*. Cambridge: Harvard University Press.

Panzarino, C. (1994). *The me in the mirror*. Seattle, WA: Seal Press.

Park, C. C. (2001). *Exiting nirvana: A daughter's life with autism*. Boston: Little, Brown.

Redfield Jamison, K. (2011). *An unquiet mind: A memoir of moods and madness*. New York: Vintage Books.

Robison, J. E. (2007). *Look me in the eye: My life with Asperger's*. New York: Random House.

Rodis, P., Garrod, A., & Boscardin, M. L. (Eds.) (2001). *Learning disabilities and life stories*. Needham Heights, MA: Allyn & Bacon.

Schmitt, A. (1994). *Brilliant idiot: An autobiography of a dyslexic*. Intercourse, PA: Good Books.

Solomon, A. (2013). *Far from the tree: Parents, children, and the search for identity*. New York: Scribner.

Stewart, J. (1989). *The body's memory*. New York: St. Martin's Press.

Wright, M. (1999). *Sounds like home: Growing up black and deaf in the South*. Washington, DC: Gallaudet University Press.

APPENDIX B: USEFUL WEBSITES

The following list is a selection of webpages that related to the content of this book. They range from curriculum materials to disability activism, from collaborative teaching practices to disability studies resources.

http://projectchoices.org/
Illinois' response to inclusion in Least Restrictive Environment

http://kidstogether.org/
Pennsylvania-based organization on Least Restrictive Environment issues

http://teachingld.org/about/
Teachers of students with learning disabilities

http://www.kotb.com
Kids on the Block. Disability awareness life-size puppet presentations for elementary schools

http://www.casel.org
Social and emotional learning for students, preschool to high school

http://www.powerof2.org/
Focus on teacher collaboration

http://www.gse.harvard.edu/news/features/speced03022001.html
Special education and civil rights

http://www.cldinternational.org/
Council for learning disabilities

http://www.disabilityfilms.co.uk/
Disability-related films (commercial and documentary)

http://www.cds.hawaii.edu/
Review of Disability Studies

http://www.digital-disability.com/
Digital Disability

http://www.columbia.edu/cu/seminars/seminars/cultural-studies/seminar-folder/disability-
    studies.html
Disability Studies seminars at Columbia University, open to the public

http://www.dsq-sds.org/
Disability Studies quarterly electronic journal

http://www.bioethicsanddisability.org/abuseofdisabledpeople.htm
Issues of abuse of disabled people

http://www.disabilitystudiesforteachers.org/
Disability studies for teachers (curricula and materials)

http://disstudies.org/
Society for Disability Studies

http://www.disabilityisnatural.com/
Disability is natural

http://www.inclusion.com/inclusionpress.html
Inclusion Press

http://www.inclusiondaily.com/
International Disability Rights New Service

http://www.ragged-edge-mag.com/0903/0903ft1.html
Alternatives to disability simulations

http://idea.ed.gov/
Building the legacy of IDEA

http://www.disabilityworld.org/
Disability World webzine

http://www.jonathanmooney.com/
Author and Public Speaker/Learning Disorder and ADHD

http://www.wholeschooling.net/
Whole schooling consortium

http://dha.osu.edu/
Disability History Association

http://www.museumofdisability.org/
Museum of Disability

http://www.cec.sped.org//AM/Template.cfm?Section=Home
Council for Exceptional Children

http://www.aera.net/SIG143/DisabilityStudiesinEducationSIG143/tabid/12121/Default.aspx
American Education Research Association/Disability Studies in Education

REFERENCES

Advocates for Children (2005). *Leaving school empty handed: A report of graduation and drop out rates for students who receive special education services in New York City.* Retrieved November 11, 2011 from *www.advocatesforchildren.org/pubs/2005/ spedgradrates.pdf*

Anastasiou, D., & Kauffman, J. M. (2011). A social constructionist approach to disability: Implications for special education. *Exceptional Children, 77*(3), 367–384.

Andrews, J. E., Carnine, D. W., Coutinho, M. J., Edgar, E. B., Forness, S. R., Fuchs, L., et al. (2000). Bridging the special education divide. *Remedial and Special Education, 21*(5), 258–260, 267.

Artiles, A., Kozleski, E., & Waitoller, F. R. (Eds.) (2011). *Inclusive education: Examining equity on five continents.* Cambridge, MA: Harvard Education Press.

Artiles, A., Rueda, R., Salazar, J. J., & Higareda, I. (2002). English language learner representation in special education in California urban school districts. In D. J. Losen & G. Orfield (Eds.), *Racial inequality in special education* (pp. 117–136). Cambridge, MA: Harvard Education Press.

Asch, A. (2001). Critical race theory, feminism, and disability: Reflections on social justice and personal identity. *Ohio State Law Journal, 62* (1), 391–423.

Ayala, E. C. (1999). "Poor little things" ind "brave little souls": The portrayal of individuals with disabilities in children's literature. *Reading Research and Instruction, 39*(1), 103–116.

Baker, B. (2002). The hunt for disability: The new eugenics and the normalization of school children. *Teachers College Record, 104,* 663–703.

Bang, M. (2004). *When Sophie gets angry—really, really angry.* New York, NY: Scholastic Paperbacks.

Bar On, B. A. (Ed.) (1993). *Modern engendering: Critical feminist readings in modern western philosophy.* Albany, New York: SUNY Press.

Brantlinger, E. (2006). The big glossies: How textbooks structure (special) education. In E. Brantlinger (Ed.), *Who benefits from special education?: Remediating (fixing) other people's children* (pp. 45–75). Mahwah, NJ: Lawrence Erlbaum.

Broderick, A., & Ne'eman, A. (2008). Autism as metaphor: Narrative and counter-narrative. *International Journal of Inclusive Education, 12*(5–6), 459–476.

Burghstaler, S. (1999). Research connections. *Council for Exceptional Children, (5)*, 2.

Charlton, J. I. (2000). *Nothing about us without us.* Berkeley, CA: University of California Press.

Children's Defense Fund (2007). *America's cradle to prison pipeline.* Washington, DC.

Cohen, R. (2001). (Director) *Going to School (Ir a la Escuela).* [Motion picture]. Los Angeles, CA: Richard Cohen films. Available at www.richardcohenfilms.com

Connor, D. J., & Bejoian, L. (2006). Pigs, pirates, and pills: Using film to teach the social context of disability. *Teaching Exceptional Children, 39*(2), 52–60.

Cuban, L. (1993). *How teachers taught: Constancy and change in American classrooms 1890–1990* (2nd ed.). New York: Teachers College Press.

Danforth, S. (2009). *The incomplete child: An intellectual history of learning disabilities.* New York: Peter Lang.

Davis, L. J. (2002). *Bending over backwards: Disability, dismodernism, and other difficult positions.* New York: New York University Press.

Deutsch, M. (1975). Equity, equality, and need: What determines which values will be used as the basis of distributive justice? *Journal of Social Issues, 31*, 137–149.

Diagnostic and Statistical Manual of Mental Disorders-IV (1994). Washington, DC: American Psychiatric Publishing.

Dudley-Marling, C., & Gurn, A. (Eds.) (2011). *The myth of the normal curve.* New York: Peter Lang.

Dunn, L. M. (1968). Education for the mentally retarded: Is much of it justifiable? *Exceptional Children, 35*(1), 5–22.

Education for All Handicapped Children Act, P.L. 94–142 (1975).

Ferri, B. A., & Connor, D. J. (2005). Tools of exclusion: Race, disability, and (re)segregated education. *Teachers College Record, 107*(3), 453–474.

Fine, M., & Asch, A. (2003). Disability beyond stigma: Social interaction, discrimination, and activism. *Journal of Social Issues, 44*(1), 3–21.

Fleischer, D. Z., & Zames, F. (2001). *The disabilities rights movement: From charity to confrontation.* Philadelphia: Temple University Press.

Friend, M., & Bursuck, W. (2011). *Including students with special needs: A practical guide for classroom teachers* (5th ed.). Upper Saddle River, NJ: Pearson.

Gabel, S. L., Curcic, S., Powell, J., Khader, K., & Albee, L. (2009). Migration and ethnic group disproportionality in special education: An exploratory study. *Disability and Society, 24*(5), 625–639.

Gabel, S. L., & Peters, S. (2004). Presage of a paradigm shift? Beyond the social model of disability toward a resistance theory of disability. *Disability and Society, 19*(6), 571–596.

Gallagher, D. J. (2004). Preface. In D. J. Gallagher, L. Heshusius, R. P. Iano & T. M. Skrtic (Eds.), *Challenging orthodoxy in special education: Dissenting voices* (pp. vii–x). Denver, CO: Love Publishing.

Gallagher, D. J., Heshusius, L., Iano, P., & Skrtic, T. M. (2004). *Challenging orthodoxy in special education: Dissenting voices.* Denver, CO: Love Publishing.

Gately, S., & Gately, J. (2001). Understanding co-teaching components. *TEACHING Exceptional Children, 33*(4), 40–47.

Goffman, E. (1963). *Stigma: Notes on the management of spoiled identity.* New York: Simon & Schuster.

Goodwin, T. C., & Wurzburg, G. (1992). (Producer and Director) Home Box Office, HBO Project Knowledge, & Ambrose Video Publishing. *Educating Peter.* New York: Ambrose Video Publishing.

Gregg, N. (2007). Underserved and unprepared: Postsecondary learning disabilities. *Learning Disabilities Research & Practice, 22*(4), 219–228.

Habib, D. (2008). (Producer and Director). *Including Samuel*. [DVD]. Available from http://www.includingsamuel.com/home.aspx

Habib, D. (2012). (Producer and Director). *Who cares about Kelsey?* [DVD]. Available from http://www.whocaresaboutkelsey.com/

Haddon, M. (2003). *The curious incident of the dog in the night-time*. Glens Falls, NY: Vintage Books.

Hehir, T. (2002). Eliminating ableism in education [Electronic version]. *Harvard Educational Review* 72. Retrieved September 30, 2004 from http://gseweb.harvard.edu/~hepg/hehir.htm

Hehir, T. (2011). *Universally designed schools that work*. Presentation at the 26th Annual Learning Differences Conference, Harvard School of Education.

Hehir, T., Figueroa, R., Gamm, S., Katzman, L. I., Gruner, A., Karger, J., & Hernandez, J. (2005). *Comprehension management review and evaluation of special education submitted to the New York City Department of Education*. Cambridge, MA: Harvard School of Education.

Individuals with Disabilities Education Act, P.L. 101–476 (1990).

Individuals with Disabilities Education Act, P.L. 105–17 (1997).

Individuals with Disabilities Education Improvement Act, P.L. 108–446 (2004).

Karagiannis, A. (2000). Soft disability in schools: Assisting or confining at risk children and youth? *Journal of Educational Thought*, *34*(2), 113–134.

Kauffman, J. M., & Hallahan, D. P. (Eds.) (1995). *The illusion of full inclusion: A comprehensive critique of a current special education bandwagon*. Austin, TX: ProEd.

Kent, E. G. (1996). (Producer and Director). *I have Tourette's but Tourette's doesn't have me: Dispelling the myth one child at a time*. New York: Home Box Office.

Kim, C., Losen, D., & Hewitt, D. (2010). *The school-to-prison pipeline: Structuring legal reform*. New York: New York University Press.

Levine, M. (1999). *Keeping ahead in school: A student's book about learning abilities and learning disorders*. Cambridge, MA: Educator's Publishing Service.

Linton, S. (1998). *Claiming Disability*. New York: New York University Press.

Liston, D., & Zeichner, K. (1996). *Culture and teaching*. Mahwah, NJ: Lawrence Erlbaum.

Liston, D., & Zeichner, K. (1991). *Teacher education and the social conditions of schooling*. New York: Routledge.

Longmore, P. (2003). *Why I burned my book and other essays on disability*. Philadelphia, PA: Temple University Press.

Losen, D., & Orfield, G. (2002). *Racial inequity in special education*. Cambridge, MA: Harvard Education Press.

Maher, F., & Ward, J. (2002). *Gender and teaching*. Mahwah, NJ: Lawrence Erlbaum.

Moxley, D., & Finch, J. (Eds.) (2003). *Sourcebook of rehabilitation and mental health practice*. New York City: Plenum.

Murawski, W. W., & Dieker, L. (2008). 50 ways to keep your co-teacher: Strategies before, during, and after co-teaching. *TEACHING Exceptional Children*, *40*(4), 40–48.

Oliver, M. (1996). Understanding the hegemony of disability. In M. Oliver (Ed.), *Understanding disability: From theory to practice* (pp. 126–144). New York: St. Martin's Press.

Postman, N. (1995). *The end of education*. New York: Knopf.

Rauscher, L., & McClintock, J. (1996). Ableism and curriculum design. In M. Adams, L. A. Bell & P. Griffen (Eds.), *Teaching for diversity and social justice* (pp. 198–231). New York: Routledge.

Rodis, P., Garrod, A., & Boscardin, M. L. (Eds.) (2001). *Learning disabilities and life stories*. Needham Heights, MA: Allyn & Bacon.

Russell, M. (1998). *Beyond ramps: Disability at the end of the social construct*. Monroe, ME: Common Courage.

Safran, S. P. (1998a). The first century of disability portrayal in film: An analysis of the literature. *Journal of Special Education, 31*(4), 467–479.

Safran, S. P. (1998b). Disability portrayal in film: Reflecting the past, directing the future. *Exceptional Children, 64*(2), 227–238.

Salend, S. (2010). *Creating inclusive classrooms: Effective and reflective practices for all students* (7th ed.). Upper Saddle River, NJ: Pearson.

Sapon-Shevin, M. (2000/2010). *Because we can change the world: A practical guide to building cooperative, inclusive classroom communities.* Thousand Oaks, CA: SAGE.

Shapiro, A. (1999). *Everybody belongs: Changing negative attitudes toward classmates with disabilities.* New York: Routledge.

Shapiro, J. (1993). *No pity: People with disabilities forging a new civil rights movement.* New York: Three Rivers Press.

Skrtic, T. M. (1991). *Behind special education: A critical analysis of professional culture and school organization.* Denver, CO: Love Publishing.

Smith, P. (Ed.) (2010). *Whatever happened to inclusion?* New York: Peter Lang.

Solomon, A. (2013). *Far from the tree: Parents, children, and the search for identity.* New York: Scribner.

Thurlow, M. L., Sinclair, M. F., & Johnson, D. R. (2002). Students with disabilities who drop out of school—Implications for policy and practice. *Issue Brief, 1*(2). Minneapolis, MN: University of Minnesota, Institute on Community Integration, National Center on Secondary Education and Transition. Retrieved November 23, 2011, from http://www.ncset.org/publications/viewdesc.asp?id=425

Tomlinson, C. A. (1999). *The differentiated classroom: Responding to the needs of all learners.* Alexandria, VA: ASCD.

Tomlinson, C. A. (2001). *How to differentiate instruction in mixed ability classrooms.* Alexandria, VA: ASCD.

Udvari-Solner, A., & Kluth, P. (2008). *Joyful learning: Active and collaborative learning in inclusive classrooms.* Thousand Oaks, CA: Corwin Press.

U.S. Department of Education (2005). *Comparative indicators of education in the United States and other G8 countries: 2004.* National Center for Education Statistics 2005–021. Retrieved November 25, 2011 from http://nces.ed.gov/pubs2007/2007006.pdf

Valle, J. W. (2009). *What mothers say about special education: From the 1960s to the present.* New York, NY: Palgrave.

Valle, J. W., & Connor, D. J. (2010). *Rethinking disability: A disability studies approach to inclusive practices.* New York: McGraw-Hill.

Vygotsky, L. S. (1987). *The collected works of L. S. Vygotsky: Problems of general psychology.* New York: Plenum Press.

Wang, M. C., Reynolds, M. C., & Walberg, H. J. (1986). Rethinking special education. *Educational Leadership, 44*(1), 26–31.

Welch, A. B. (2000). Responding to student concerns about fairness. *Exceptional Children, 33*(2), 36–40.

Wendell, S. (2000). The social construction of disability. In M. Adams, W. Blumenfeld, C. Castaneda, H. Hackman, M. Peters & X. Zuniga (Eds.), *Readings for diversity and social justice* (pp. 477–481). New York: Routledge.

Wurzburg, G. (2001). (Director and Producer). *Graduating Peter.* [Motion Picture]. New York: Home Box Office.

Zinn, H. (2005). *A people's history of the United States: 1492 – present* (2nd ed.). New York: Harper Perennial.

INDEX

Taylor & Francis

eBooks

FOR LIBRARIES

ORDER YOUR
FREE 30 DAY
INSTITUTIONAL
TRIAL TODAY!

Over 23,000 eBook titles in the Humanities,
Social Sciences, STM and Law from some of the
world's leading imprints.

Choose from a range of subject packages or create your own!

▶ Free MARC records
▶ COUNTER-compliant usage statistics
▶ Flexible purchase and pricing options

▶ Off-site, anytime access via Athens or referring URL
▶ Print or copy pages or chapters
▶ Full content search
▶ Bookmark, highlight and annotate text
▶ Access to thousands of pages of quality research
　at the click of a button

For more information, pricing enquiries or to order
a free trial, contact your local online sales team.

UK and Rest of World: **online.sales@tandf.co.uk**
US, Canada and Latin America:
e-reference@taylorandfrancis.com

www.ebooksubscriptions.com

A flexible and dynamic resource for teaching, learning and research.